THE CHURCH RECORDS OF SAINT MATTHEW'S LUTHERAN CHURCH ORANGEBURG COUNTY, SOUTH CAROLINA AND "THE RED CHURCH"

BY
ANNE MARTIN HAIGLER

Copyright 1985
By: Southern Historical Press, Inc.

All rights reserved. No part of this publication may be reproduced,
stored in a retrieval system, transmitted in any form,
posted on to the web in any form or by any means
without the prior written permission of the publisher.

Please direct all correspondence and orders to:

www.southernhistoricalpress.com
or
**SOUTHERN HISTORICAL PRESS, Inc.
PO BOX 1267
375 West Broad Street
Greenville, SC 29601
southernhistoricalpress@gmail.com**

ISBN #0-89308-563-4

Printed in the United States of America

INTRODUCTION

This book contains church records from two St. Matthew's churches in the Orangeburg, South Carolina, area: St. Matthew's Lutheran Church in Orangeburg, and the other St. Matthew's Episcopal Church in Fort Motte, S.C., also known as "The Red Church."

Mrs. Haigler transcribed the records of the St. Matthew's Lutheran Church from the original record book in the South Caroliniana Library, Columbia, S.C. For some reason the original records of "The Red Church" for 1767-1838 were also found in this book and these are included.

The St. Matthew's Episcopal Parish traces its beginning to a few English and French Huguenot families and many German Swiss who were living in Amelia Township, in what was then Berkeley County. The chapel was built in 1757 and the Parish was established in 1765 extending from Nelson's Ferry (above Eutawville) to Beaver Creek and from the Santee and Congaree rivers to the Edisto River. The church was moved in 1800, 1815-1819 and again in 1852 when it was erected on its present site near Fort Motte.

These records from St. Matthew's Lutheran Church are going to be of utmost importance for genealogists working in Orangeburg and Lexington counties, since both are burned counties and so many of the people are found in these church registers for descendants living later in Lexington County.

FOREWORD

All information in this record enclosed in parenthesis appears to have been added to the original at a later time and is in a different handwriting.

Notice on Page 3, Line 8:
"Hannah Rast was born July 19, 1797 (B. Cummings)"

Hannah Rast did marry Benjamin Cummings so the other names in parenthesis in various places through out the record, may also be spouses names.

Also, notice on Page 3, Line 2:
"Hannah Rast his wife was born   "

No date was given for her birth so I have left the space blank.

In some places the writing was not legible to me and I have indicated this with a line and a question mark.

Rev. Paul Derrick was born in Lexington District, South Carolina August 29th A.D. 1829.

Amanda B. Derrick was born in Lexington District, South Carolina October 15th 1835.

Rev. Paul Derrick & Amanda B. Hiller were united in wedlock by Rev. Jacob Hawkins November 25th A.D. 1858.

Samuel Joseph Houck, son of Rev. Paul & Amanda B. Derrick was born in St. Matthew's Parish, South Carolina Sept. 22nd A.D. 1859.

Sidney Bartow, second son of Rev. Paul & Amanda B. Derrick, was born in St. Matthew's Parish, South Carolina Sept. 12th A.D. 1861.

Henry David, third son of Rev. Paul & Amanda B. Derrick, was born in St. Matthew's Parish, South Carolina October 10th A.D. 1863.

John Edwin, fourth son of Rev. Paul & Amanda B. Derrick, was born in St. Matthew's Parish, South Carolina January 30th A.D. 1866.

John Phillip Francklow	born July 17th, 1758
Sarah Francklow	born Nov. 1, 1759
Married	June 6th 1785
Rachell Anne Francklow	born March 14th 1786 - d. 26 May 1793
John Hepworth Francklow	born Jan 14th 1788
Sarah Frances Francklow	born Feb 25th 1790
Deborah Leah Francklow	born Jan 23rd 1794

The whole family born in the City of London in England. Emigrated from London July 19, 1796 arrived in Charleston, South Carolina Sept 16th 1796.

The Rev. John P. Francklow was, according to his own statement, ordained and licensed to preach and baptize by the Bishop of the Episcopal church residing in Charleston in 1798. He was afterwards (in 1812) licensed by the North Carolina Synod. He served this congregation from 1799 to 1814. From this time until his death in 1829 he labored in Lexington County. He joined the South Carolina Synod at its organization in 1824. His descendents still live in Lexington.

John Conrad Holman	born Sep 20, 1775
Rachell Holman	born May 26, 1790
William Conrad Holman, 1st son	born Sep 8, 1809
Eve Mary Holman, 1st dau.	born April 6th, 1811
John Russell Holman, 2nd son	born April 9th, 1813
James Thomas Holman, 3rd son	born Oct 23rd, 1814
Jessey Knodel Holman, 4th son	born Nov 27th, 1818
Elizabeth Rachel Holman	born Dec 8, 1819
Ann Catherine Holman	born Jan 22nd, 1821
John Joseph Holman	born Oct 9th, 1823
Eugenah Rebaca Holman	born Feb 11th, 1826
David Luther Holman	born June 15th, 1829

Christian Gates	born in the year 1762
Elisabeth, his wife	born Feb 7th, 1775
They were married by the Rev'd. Mr. Beniger on Jan 3, 1795	
William, their 1st son	born Nov 23rd 1797
Geo. Gates, 2nd son	born Nov 22nd, 1799

Samuel, 3rd son   born Jan 30th, 1802
Mary, 1st dau.   born Oct 26, 1804
Catherine, 2nd dau.   born Apr 20th, 1807
Elisabeth Margeret, 3rd dau.   born Jan 8th, 1811
John Christian, 4th son   born Jan 2nd, 1813

Rev. Geo. A. Hough   born Mar 8th, 1839
Sallie M. Hough   born Sep 14th, 1852
Willie Rude Hough   born Sep 13th, 1872
Russel Zimmerman   born Dec 19th, 1873

Rev. S.T. Hallman was born, in Lexington County, S.C. September 3rd, 1844.
Sarah Jane Hallman was born January 9th, 1849.
Milledge Soloman Hallman was born December 8, 1865.

Conrad Gaits   born Apr 30th, 1774
Elizabeth Gaits   born
Lewis Gaits, 1st son   born Nov 26th, 1799
Joseph Gaits, 2nd son   born Dec 24th, 1801
Harriot Gaits, 1st dau.   born Mar 11th, 1806
John M. Gaits, 3rd son   born Jan 19th, 1810
Ann M. Gaits, 2nd dau.   born Jan 19th, 1810
James Russell   born Apr 10th, 1813

John Anthony Menicken born May 15th 1785 at Cologne on the river Reihn.

Rev. J.P. Francklow

In 1812 the Synod of North Carolina requested Rev. Mr. Francklow to make one or more visits to a part of South Carolina called "Salketcher" to look up Lutherans. This he did - an abstract of his report being found in the minutes of that synod. About 1860, the original document was found among the papers of Rev. G. Shoker of N.C. and it is given entire in Rev. Bernheims "History of German Lutheran Settlements in the Carolinas" pp. 385-388.

George Roye   born Mar 7, 1779
Elisabeth Roye   born Sep 28, 1780
Married Dec 27, 1798 by William Heatly, Esq.
Maria Roy, 1st dau.   born Sep 1, 1799 - bap. Sep 29, 1799
John Aron Roy, 1st son   born Aug 10, 1800 - died Aug 1800
Jacob Martin Roy 2d son   born Aug 15, 1801 - bap. Sep 6, 1801
Perce Roy, 3rd son   born Oct 8, 1803 - bap. Nov 28, 1803
Anne Roy, 2nd dau.   born May 10, 1805
George Russel Roy, 4th son   born Sep 5, 1809
James Drane Roy, 5th son   born Sep 4, 1810

George Rast was born Apr 3, 1763
Hannah Rast his wife was born   (formerly Vice)
They was married October 3rd 1786

Elizabeth Rast was born Sep 5th 1787   (C. Whetstone)
Magdeline Rast was born Oct 8th 1789   (John Keller & Jacob
                                                        Keller)
Catherine Rast was born Apr 5th 1792   (Jacob Keller)
Margret Rast was born Jul 1st 1794   (Jacob Keller)
Hannah Rast was born Jul 19th 1797   (B. Cummings)
Mary Rast was born Jul 20th 1799   (Tilly & Dantzler)
John Adam Rast was born Jul 22nd 1802
Christina Rast was born Apr 20th 1805   (Dave Bull)

2

John D. Scheck was born Sep 23rd 1802 in the city Winchester State Virginia.
Joicee C. Scheck was born Nov 28th 1803 in Newberry District South Carolina.
Luther Whitfield Scheck their first son was born Jul 8th 1839.
Mary Ann Eliza Scheck was born Aug 12th 1831.

Rev. J. Hawkins was born Sep 4, 1828 in Newberry county S.C. son of Rev. Peter W. Hawkins and Mary, his wife.
Mary Louise Wingard, daughter of John and Sarah N. Wingard, was born Oct 17, 1834 in Lexington County, S.C.
They were married by Rev. W. Berley Nov 20, 1855.

Their Children:
(1) Mary Ella Hawkins was born Nov 18, 1856 in Lexington Co., S.C.
(2) Emma Kinard Hawkins was born Jul 14, 1859, at Beth Eden, Newberry Co., S.C.
(3) John Jacob Hawkins was born Aug 5, 1861 in Savannah, Ga.
(4) Sarah Elizabeth Hawkins was born Nov 28, 1864 in Effingham County, Georgia.
(5) Willie Schirmer Hawkins was born Nov 7, 1869 at Beth Eden, Newberry Co., S.C.
(6) Joseph Wingard Hawkins was born Mar 4, 1867 at Beth Eden, Newberry Co., S.C.
(7) Virginia Hawkins was born Jan 4, 1873 in Shepherdstown, W. Va.
(8) Charles Duval Hawkins was born May 26, 1875 in Middletown, Frederick County, Md.
(9) Helen Rude Hawkins was born Oct 26, 1878 near St. Michaels Church, Lexington Co., S.C.

Mary Ella Hawkins died Sep 5, 1857
Willie Scherimer Hawkins died Jan 16, 1870
Joseph Wingard Hawkins died at Prosperity, S.C. June 20, 1881 aged 14 yrs. 3 mos. & 16 days.
Rev. J. Hawkins died June 1895.
J.W. Selers Hawkins died Aug 1895.
Rev. Y. Holland died Oct 1895.
Mrs. Hawkins died in Virginia Dec 1904.

Childrens Names	When Christened	When Born	Parents Names
George West	April 13, 1799		son of Mr & Mrs West
Mary Elisabeth Hoffman	April 14, 1799		dau of Mr & Mrs Hoffman
Mary Weis	April 21, 1799		dau of Mr & Mrs Weis
William James Buttler	April 21, 1799		son of Mr & Mrs James Buttler
Harriet Barsh	April 24, 1799		dau of Mr & Mrs George Barsh
Charlotte Barsh	April 24, 1799		dau of John & Catherine Barsh
Mary Buttler	April 24, 1799		dau of Mr & Mrs George Buttler
William Hesse	April 24, 1799		son of Mr & Mrs Hesse
Rachell Steinwinder	April 24, 1799		dau of Mr & Mrs Frederick Steinwinder
George Arnold Campbell	April 24, 1799	Oct 2, 1792	son of Mr & Mrs George Campbell
Mary Elisabeth Campbell	April 24, 1799		dau of Mr & Mrs George Campbell
Eliza Rebecca Campbell	April 24, 1799		dau of Mr & Mrs George Campbell
John David Gates	April 28, 1799		son of Mr & Mrs Martin Gates
Mary Miegler	April 28, 1799		dau of Mr & Mrs Conrad Miegler
Catherine Seger	May 21, 1799		dau of Mr & Mrs John Seger
Maria Stoutenmeyer	June 5, 1799		dau of Mr & Mrs Martin Stoutenmeyer
Conrad Waltz	June 9, 1799		son of Mr & Mrs Casper Waltz
Joseph Rast	June 9, 1799		son of Mathias & Barbara Rast
DAvid Ziegler	June 24, 1799		son of Mr & Mrs Andrew Ziegler
Anne Felder	July 7, 1799		dau of Henry & Margaret Felder
Anne Christina Burk	July 13, 1799	May 30, 1799	dau of John Leoy & Christina Burk
Peter Fogel	Aug 4, 1799		son of Mr & Mrs Anthony Fogel
Mary Rast	Aug 12, 1799		dau of George & Hannah Rast
Michial Theus	Sep 1, 1799		son of Mr & Mrs Simon Theus
Maria Roy	Sep 29, 1799	Sep 1, 1799	dau of George & Elizabeth Roy
Frederick Rast) twins	Oct 27, 1799		son of Mr & Mrs John Rast
Conrad Rast)	Oct 27, 1799		son of Mr & Mrs John Rast
Elisabeth King	Nov 10, 1799	Oct 26, 1799	dau of Mr & Mrs Christopher King
Aron Keller	Nov 17, 1799		son of Mr & Mrs Jacob Keller
John Martin Stoutenmeyer	Dec 8, 1799		son of Mr & Mrs Mathias Stoutenmeyer
Ludwig Gates	Dec 14, 1799		son of Conrad & Elisabeth Gates
John Martin Gates	Dec 22, 1799		
Andrew Stabler	Dec 25, 1799		son of Mr & Mrs John Stabler
Mary Stabler	Dec 25, 1799		dau of Mr & Mrs Jacob Stabler
John Zimmerman	Dec 25, 1799		son of Mr & Mrs Adam Zimmerman
Joseph Sellars	Feb 5, 1800		son of Mr & Mrs Martin Sellars
Robert Watts	Mar 29, 1800		son of Mr & Mrs John Watts
Elisabeth Isabelle Axton	Mar 29, 1800		dau of Mr & Mrs John Axton

Childrens Names	When Born	When Christened	Parents Names
John Hoffman		Mar 30, 1800	son of John & Barbara Hoffman
Mary Shirer		May 22, 1800	son of Mr & Mrs Paul Shirer
John Herman		June 1, 1800	son of Mr & Mrs Philip Herman
John Frederick de Bardeleben		June 1, 1800	son of Margaret & Arthur de Bardeleben
Elizabeth Ryser		June 22, 1800	dau of Mr & Mrs Joseph Riser
Sarah Genoble		June 22, 1800	dau of Mr & Mrs Genoble
Hannah Zimmerman		June 22, 1800	dau of Mr & Mrs Zimmerman
William Hair		June 29, 1800	son of Conrad & Margeret Hair
John Aron Roy	Aug 10, 1800	Aug 10, 1800	son of George & Elizabeth Roy
David Gates		Aug 17, 1800	son of
John Sellars		Aug 17, 1800	son of Mr & Mrs Andrew Sellars
Elisa Boshett		Sep 14, 1800	dau of Mr & Mrs Wm. Boshatt
Elizabeth Pein		Sep 14, 1800	dau of Mr & Mrs Frederick Pein
Mary Axton	Oct 4, 1800	Oct 19, 1800	dau of Mr & Mrs Axton
Magdalen Ziegler		Nov 16, 1800	dau of Mr & Mrs John Ziegler
Nuel Stoutenmyer		Dec 14, 1800	son of John & Jennett Stoutenmyer
Henry Olliver		Jan 4, 1801	son of Mr & Mrs Olliver of Beaver Creek
David Ziegler		Jan 4, 1801	son of Mr & Mrs Geo. Ziegler of Beaver Creek
Elisabeth Stabler		Jan 4, 1801	dau of Mr & Mrs Stabler of Beaver Creek
Mary Steinwinder		Jan 4, 1801	dau of Mr & Mrs Fredk Steinwinder of BeaverCr
Ludwig Shepherd		Jan 14, 1801	son of Mr & Mrs Shepherd
Mary Elisabeth Austin		Jan 16, 1801	dau of William & Mary Austin
Mary Buttler, wife of Chas Buttler		Jan 21, 1801	
Elisabeth Buttler, sister of Chas Buttler		Jan 21, 1801	
Thomas Buttler, bro. of Chas Buttler		Jan 21, 1801	
Thomas Buttler		Jan 21, 1801	son of Charles & Mary Buttler
James Buttler		Jan 21, 1801	son of Charles & Mary Buttler
Eugina Holman		Jan 28, 1801	dau of Melchoir & Mary Holman
Danniel Hoffman		Feb 6, 1801	son of John Andrew & Mary Hoffman
William Zimmerman		Feb 9, 1801	son of Daniel & Elisabeth Zimmerman
Samuel Switzer		Feb 16, 1801	son of Mr & Mrs Henry Switzer
Emma Cassia Hart		Feb 17, 1801	dau of Benjamin Hart, Esq.
Alexander Gillon Nixon		Feb 21, 1801	son of Nixon Esq. of Beaver Creek
Samuel Corbyn		Feb 22, 1801	son of Mr & Mrs Samuel Corbyn of Beaver Cr.
Catherine Stabler		Feb 22, 1801	dau of Mr & Mrs Andrew Stabler of Beaver Cr.
Jacob Brandeburg		Mar 11, 1801	son of Mr & Mrs Martin Brandeburg
David Rast		Mar 25, 1801	son of Mr & Mrs Frederick Rast
William George Myers		Mar 22, 1801	son of Mr & Mrs David Myers

Childrens Names	When Born	When Christened	Parents Names
Chrissie Thomson		April 1, 1801	dau of Dorothy Thomson
Carolina Burkett		April 22, 1801	dau of John & Juliana Burkett
Hannah Stoutenmyer		May 10, 1801	dau of Mat & Barbara Stoutenmyer
Catherine Lucretia Miegler		May 22, 1801	dau of Mr & Mrs Conrad Miegler
Ludwig Felder		June 13, 1801	son of Henry & Margaret Felder
Anna Genoble		July 6, 1801	dau of Mr & Mrs Genoble
Margaret Burkett		Aug 2, 1801	dau of Mr & Mrs Casper Burkett
John David Fitzpatrick	Aug 15, 1801	Aug 16, 1801	son of Rosina Fitzpatrick
Jacob Martin Roy		Sep 6, 1801	son of George & Elizabeth Roy
Catherine Ziegler		Sep 17, 1801	dau of Mr & Mrs Aw Zielger
Rosina Keller		Oct 4, 1801	dau of Jacob & Susanna Keller
Robert Miller		Nov 14, 1801	son of Mr & Mrs Miller
Elisabeth Catherine Houser		Nov 29, 1801	dau of Mr & mrs C. Houser
Rosina Catherine Hair		Nov 29, 1801	dau of Mr & Mrs Hair
John Rudolph Beck		Dec 6, 1801	son of Mrs Beck
Mary Waltz		Dec 25, 1801	dau of Mr & Mrs Casr Waltz
William James Stoutenmyer		Jan 3, 1802	son of Mr & Mrs Geo. Stoutenmyer
Peter Garick		Jan 8, 1802	son of John & Catherine Garick
DAvid GArick		Jan 9, 1802	son of Mr & Mrs Adam Garick
Joseph Gates		Jan 17, 1802	son of Conrad & Elisabeth Gates
----- Hoffman		Feb 27, 1802	dau of John & Barbara Hoffman
Samuel Gates	Jan 30, 1802	Feb 29, 1802	son of Christian & Elisabeth Gates
Moses Robert Livingston		Mar 29, 1802	son of Mr & Mrs William Livingston
Samuel Sellers		Apr 11, 1802	son of Mr & Mrs Martin Sellers
Maria Lousiana Stoutenmyer		Aug 8, 1802	dau of John & Elisabeth Stoutenmyer
John Adam Rast		Aug 22, 1802	son of George & Hannah Rast
William Robert Irick		Sep 1, 1802	son of Valentine & Maria Gates
William Arthur Bardelaben		Sep 5, 1802	son of Arthur & Margaret Bardelaben
Anne Sussana Riser		Sep 5, 1802	dau of Mr & mrs Joseph Riser
Rebecca Hoffman		Oct 14, 1802	dau of John & Elisabeth Hoffman
John Conrad Zimmerman		Oct 17, 1802	son of Daniel & Elisabeth Zimmerman
Martin Hair		Oct 31, 1802	son of Conrad & Elisabeth Hair
Magdelan Harman		Oct 31, 1802	dau of Mr & Mrs Philip Harmon
Adam Buttler		Nov 13, 1802	son of Mr & Mrs George Buttler
Ludwig Buttler		Nov 13, 1802	son of Mr & Mrs George Buttler
Maria Stabler) twins		Dec 1, 1802	dau of Mr & Mrs Fred Stabler
Anne Stabler)		Dec 1, 1802	dau of Mr & Mrs Fred Stabler
John James Haigler		Dec 9, 1802	son of Henry & Mary Haigler

Childrens Names	When Born	When Christened	Parents Names
Rosina Keller		Dec 18, 1802	dau of Jacob & Susanna Keller
John Adam Genoble		Dec 20, 1802	son of John & Margaret Genoble
William Robert Hoffman		Jan 10, 1803	son of John A. & Mary Hoffman
Charles Shadrack Austin		Jan 10, 1803	son of Sarah Bond
Adam Rast) twins Eve Rast)		Feb 13, 1803	son & dau of Mr & Mrs John Rast
Adam Melchior Holman		Mar 9, 1803	son of Melchior & Mary Holman
William Slater		April 27, 1803	son of Mr & Mrs Slater
Henry Switzer		May 1, 1803	son of Mr & Mrs Switzer
Christina Barbour		May 14, 1803	dau of Mr & Mrs George Barbour
Maria Ziegler		June 5, 1803	dau of Mr & Mrs John Ziegler
Rebecca Felder		June 26, 1803	dau of Henry & Margaret Felder
Elisabeth Mary McCord		July 10, 1803	
Sophia Anne McCord		July 10, 1803	daus of Mr & Mrs Joseph McCord
Mary Hair		Aug 7, 1803	dau of Mr & Mrs James Hair
Ephraim King		Sep 28, 1803	son of Mr & Mrs Christopher King
Edmon Slater	Aug 26, 1803	Oct 2, 1803	dau of Mr & Mrs Slater
Eve Garick		Oct 7, 1803	dau of Mr & Mrs John Garick
SAmuel Stabler		Oct 9, 1803	son of Mr & Mrs Christian Stabler
John Jacob Syfrid		Oct 9, 1803	son of Mr & Mrs Thomas Syfrid
Barbara Murph		Oct 23, 1803	dau of Rudolph & Jane Murph
Harriet Meigler		Nov 11, 1803	dau of Mr & Mrs Conrad Meigler
Harriet Fogel		Nov 14, 1803	dau of Rachel Fogel
Anne Barsh		Nov 14, 1803	dau of John & Catherine Barsh
Pearce Roy	Oct 8, 1803	Nov 28, 1803	son of Geo. & Elisabeth Roy
Alexander Steinwinder		Jan 1, 1804	son of Mr & Mrs Fredk Steinwinder
John Ziegler		Jan 1, 1804	son of Mr & Mrs Geo. Ziegler
Juliana Stoutenmyer		Jan 19, 1804	dau of John & Jennett Stoutenmyer
Richard Henry Huber		Jan 19, 1804	son of Mr & Mrs Jacob Huber
Henry Sauerhafin		Jan 21, 1804	son of Conrad & Elisabeth Sauerhafin
Conrad Brandeburg		Jan 21, 1804	son of Mr & Mrs Marn Brandeburg
John Rast		Jan 21, 1804	son of Mathias & Barbara Rast
Martin Sellers		Jan 29, 1804	son of Mr & Mrs Martin Sellers
Juliana Stoutenmyer		Feb 11, 1804	dau of Mathias & Barb. Stoutenmyer
----- Keller		Feb 11, 1804	son of Jacob & Christina Keller
Barbara Brandeburg		Mar 4, 1804	dau of Martin & C. Brandeburg
John Martin Stoutenmyer		Mar 4, 1804	son of Mr & Mrs Geo. Stoutenmyer
----- Livingston		Mar 9, 1804	son of Mr & Mrs Wm. Livingston

7

Childrens Names	When Born	When Christened	Parents Names
Catherine Hoffman		Feb 11, 1804	dau of John & E. Hoffman
Anne Maria Sellers		June 20, 1804	dau of Mr & Mrs A. Sellers
Elisa Genoble		July 8, 1804	dau of John & M. Genoble
John Alexander Irick		July 21, 1804	son of Mr & Mrs Valentine Irick
Rosina Stifflemyer		July 21, 1804	dau of Mr & Mrs Jno. Stifflemyer
Henry Rast		July 22, 1804	son of Mr & Mrs Conrad Rast
John Fredk Rast		July 29, 1804	son of Mr & Mrs Fredk Rast
Adam Garick		July 29, 1804	son of Mr & Mrs Adam Garick
Reuben Christopher Houser		Sep 23, 1804	son of Mr & Mrs Jacob Houser
Susanna Fogel		Sep 30, 1804	dau of Mr & Mrs John Fogel
Juliana Mary Maria Meyers		Oct 14, 1804	dau of Mr & Mrs David Myers
John Henry Murph		Nov 18, 1804	son of Rudolph & Jane Murph
Catherine Barbour		Dec 2, 1804	dau of Mr & Mrs Geo. Barbour
David Hair		Dec 2, 1804	son of J. & Margaret Hair
Mary Gates	Oct 26, 1804	Dec 8, 1804	dau of Mr & Mrs Chn Gates
Melchior Holman		Dec 23, 1804	son of Melchior & Mary Holman
------		Jan 17, 1805	son of Mr & Mrs James Buttler
------		Jan 23, 1805	son of Mr & Mrs Henry Haigler
------		Feb 11, 1805	son of ------ ------
William Robert Hoffman		Mar 7, 1805	son of John & Elisabeth Hoffman
Rebecca Klein		Mar 27, 1805	dau of Mr & Mrs Klein
John Pein		May 6, 1805	son of Mr & Mrs Fredk Pein
Samuel Rast		July 6, 1805	son of Mr & Mrs John Rast
Eleanora Carolina Hair		July 13, 1805	dau of Mr & Mrs Peter Hair
John Ballard		July 23, 1805	son of Mr & Mrs Ballard
------		July 23, 1805	dau of Mr & Mrs Aw Ziegler
Rosina Brandeburg		Aug 18, 1805	dau of Mr & Mrs M. Brandeburg
Elisabeth Eleanora Huber		Oct 26, 1805	dau of Jacob & Elisabeth Huber
Francis Ziegler		Nov 9, 1805	dau of Geo. & R. Ziegler
Maria GArick		Dec 9, 1805	dau of John & Cath. Garick
Margaret Wannamaker		Dec 9, 1805	dau of Jacob & E. Wannamaker
Abraham Felder		Feb 15, 1806	son of Jacob & E. Houser
------		Feb 29, 1806	dau of Henry & Rebecca Felder
------		Feb 29, 1806	dau of Mr & Mrs Jno. Livingston
Elisabeth Switzer		Mar 18, 1806	dau of Mr & Mrs H. Switzer
------		Mar 22, 1806	son of John & E. Ziegler
William Sager		Mar 22, 1806	son of Mr & Mrs John Seger

Childrens Names	When Born	When Christened	Parents Names
John Brandeburg		Apr 3, 1806	son of Martin & Cathe Brandeburg
Harriet Gates		Apr 3, 1806	dau of Mr & Mrs Conrad Gates
Rachell Rickenbaker		Apr 11, 1806	dau of Mr & Mrs Rickenbaker
Sarah Ziegler		Apr 25, 1806	dau of Jacob Ziegler of Beaver Creek
Barbara Ulmer	Apr 18, 1806	June 1, 1806	dau of Fredk & Cathe Ulmer
Mary Martha Irick		June 20, 1806	dau of Valentine & Mary Irick
Sarah Elisabeth Austin	Aug 8, 1806	Aug 17, 1806	dau of William & Mary Austin
Eliza Rast		Sep 1, 1806	dau of Mr & Mrs Conrad Rast
Anne Margaret Bardaleben		Sep 4, 1806	dau of Margaret & ARthur Bardaleben
Charles Frederick Buttler		Sep 4, 1806	son of Mr & Mrs George Buttler
Elisa Fogel		Sep 7, 1806	dau of John & Magdelen Fogel
Elisa Meyers	Jan 23, 1806	Sep 10, 1806	dau of David & Elisabeth Meyers
Catherine Stoutenmyer	Aug 18, 1806	Oct 4, 1806	dau of Mr & Mrs Mat Stoutenmyer
Rebecca Meigler		Oct 19, 1806	dau of Mr & Mrs Conrad Meigler
Elisabeth Rast		Nov 16, 1806	dau of Mr & Mrs Mathias Rast
Geo. Henry Barsh	Aug 25, 1806	Nov 23, 1806	son of John & Catherine Barsh
Elisabeth Burkett	Oct 25, 1806	Dec 1, 1806	dau of Mr & Mrs Casper Burkett
ADam Pein	Oct 30, 1806	Dec 7, 1806	son of Mr & Mrs Fredk Pein
Anne Rebecca Boshett	Nov 14, 1806	Dec 19, 1806	dau of Mr & Mrs William Boskett
John Hair		Dec 26, 1806	son of Mr & Mrs James Hair
George Hoffman		Dec 26, 1806	son of John A. & Mary Hoffman
David Hair	Nov 17, 1806	Jan 10, 1807	son of Jacob Hair & Margaret Fogel
Anne Slater		Jan 12, 1807	dau of Jane Slater
Harriet Rebecca Bonds		Apr 13, 1807	dau of Sarah Bonds
Martin Nepolitan Wannamacker	Sep 12, 1806	May 3, 1807	son of Jacob & Elisabeth Wannamaker
Charles Alexander) Mackiny Anne Christina) Elisabeth		June 16, 1807	son & dau of Mr & Mrs Mackiny, all of Mile Branch
Josiah Ziegler		June 16, 1807	son of Mr & Mrs Geo. Ziegler, Mile Branch
Jane Sarah LIvingston	June 16, 1807	July 17, 1807	dau of Mr & Mrs Wm. Livingston
Catherine Gates	Apr 20, 1807	July 26, 1807	dau of Mr & Mrs Christian Gates
Alexander Stabler		Aug 1, 1807	son of Mr & Mrs Jacob Stabler, Beaver Creek
Harriet Stabler		Aug 1, 1807	dau of Mr & Mrs Fredk Stabler
Harriet Carolina Bardaleben	July 29, 1807	Aug 14, 1807	dau of Arthur & Mary Bardaleben
Mary Shull	June 20, 1807	Sep 16, 1807	dau of Rachell Troutman
William James Smith		Sep 27, 1807	son of Mr & Mrs Jacob Smith
Elisabeth Barbour		Oct 11, 1807	dau of
Christina Anne Stabler		Oct 24, 1807	dau of Mr & Mrs Chn. Stabler, Beaver Creek

Childrens Names	When Born	When Christened	Parents Names
Abednego Felkel		Dec 6, 1807	son of Mr & Mrs Felkel
Jacob Stoutenmyer		Dec 21, 1807	son of Jacob & Margaret Stoutenmyer
Andrew Haigler		Dec 21, 1807	son of Mr & Mrs Frederick Haigler
Joseph David Keller		Feb 5, 1808	son of Mr & Mrs Keller
Adam Stiffelmyer		Feb 12, 1808	son of Mr & Mrs John Stiffelmyer
Louisa de Bardaleben		Mar 27, 1808	dau of Arthur & Margaret Bardaleben
Nicolas Ziegler		Apr 16, 1808	son of Mr & Mrs Jacob Ziegler, Beaver Creek
Simeon Speignard		Apr 16, 1808	son of Mr & Mrs Geo. Speignard, Beaver Cr.
John Ziegler		Apr 17, 1808	son of Geo. & Rachell Ziegler
Ludwig Brandeburg		Apr 24, 1808	son of Mr & Mrs Martin Brandeburg
William Jacob Weis		May 15, 1808	son of Magdelen Weis
George Noah Barsh		May 29, 1808	son of Christina Sellers
Samuel Livingston		June 4, 1808	son of Mr & Mrs John Livingston
Catherine Pein		June 22, 1808	dau of Mr & Mrs Frederick Pein
Mary Dorcas Burchmore)	Sep 22, 1807	July 4, 1808	son & dau of Mr & Mrs Burchmore
William Johnson Burchmore)		July 17, 1808	son of Frederick & Rosina Gates
Martin Gates		Aug 1, 1808	son of George & Anne Smoak
Adam SMoak		Aug 8, 1808	son of Mr & Mrs John Fogel
Jacob Fogel		Sep 7, 1808	son of John & Elisabeth Meyers
John Meyers		Dec 4, 1808	dau of Valentine & Mary Irick
Charlotte Louisa Irick		Jan 1, 1809	son of Mr & Mrs Henry Haigler
Josiah Haigler		Jan 1, 1809	son of Mr & Mrs Mathias SToutenmyer
William SToutenmyer		Jan 8, 1809	son of Mr & Mrs Martin Brandeburg
David Brandeburg		Jan 26, 1809	dau of Mr & Mrs George Barbour
----- Barbour		Feb 3, 1809	son of Mr & Mrs Adam Garick
----- Garick		Feb 10, 1809	son of Mr & Mrs Conrad Rast
----- Rast		FEb 17, 1809	dau of Jacob & Elisabeth Wannamaker
Anne Eugina Wannamaker		Feb 17, 1809	son of Mr & Mrs Adam Haigler
----- Haigler		Feb 19, 1809	dau of Mr & Mrs John Ziegler
Elisabeth Ziegler		Feb 19, 1809	dau of Mr & Mrs John Stiffelmyer
Catherine Stiffelmyer		FEb 26, 1809	son of Adam and Sophia Brandeburg
James Martin Brandburg		Mar 12, 1809	dau of Mr & Mrs Abednego Parlor
Rachell Anne Parlor		Mar 12, 1809	dau of Mr & Mrs Deleny
Carolina Anne		Mar 12, 1809	dau of Mr & Mrs John Buchard
Mary Magdelen Buchard		Mar 19, 1809	dau of Mr & Mrs Jacob Gates
Eve Matilda Gates		Apr 9, 1809	son of Mr & Mrs Struble
John Joseph Struble		Apr 12, 1809	son of John & Catherine Garick
John Garick			

Childrens Names	When Born	When Christened	Parents Names
Elizabeth Dash		May 7, 1809	dau of Mr & Mrs George Dash
Shadrach Strohman Haigler		May 7, 1809	son of Mr & Mrs Jacob Haigler
Mary Magdelen Miegler		May 14, 1809	dau of Mr & Mrs Miegler
Mary Magdelen Buchard		May 14, 1809	4 children at the Independant meeting
Martin Andrew Keller		June 11, 1809	son of Jacob & Christina Keller
Caroline Ziegler		Sep 18, 1809	dau of George & Rachel Ziegler
Rebecca Capstead		Sep 18, 1809	dau of Mr & Mrs Capstead
William Conrad Holman	Sep 8, 1809	Oct 8, 1809	son of Conrad & Rachell Holman
Adam Gates		Oct 28, 1809	son of John & Elisabeth Gates
----- Smith		Nov 15, 1809	son of Mr & Mrs Smith
Rebecca Brandeburg		Nov 15, 1809	dau of Martin & Cathe Brandeburg
Abner Utz		Jan 1, 1810	son of Mr & Mrs Geo. Utz
Elisa Sellers		Jan 20, 1810	dau of Mr & Mrs Andrew Sellers
John Martin) Gates-twins		Feb 18, 1810	son & dau of Mr & Mrs Conrad Gates
Mary Maria)			
John William Burket		Feb 20, 1810	son of Mr & Mrs Casper Burket
Eve Elisa Gates		Mar 18, 1810	dau of Fredk & Rosina Gates
Patrick Haigler		Mar 25, 1810	son of Mr & Mrs Henry Haigler
John Patrick Buttler		Apr 14, 1810	son of Mr & Mrs James Buttler
Catherine Charlotte Felkle		Apr 14, 1810	dau of Mr & Mrs Melchior Felkle
Jeremiah Morgan Haigler		Apr 22, 1810	son of Mr & Mrs Adam Haigler
William David Stiffelmyer		June 17, 1810	son of Mr & Mrs John Stiffelmyer
Sarah Segar		June 30, 1810	dau of Mr & Mrs John Segar
John Little Parler		Aug 6, 1810	son of Mr & Mrs Shadrach Parler
Carolina Smoak		Sep 22, 1810	dau of George & Anne Smoak
Eleanora		Sep 23, 1810	dau of John A. & Elisabeth Meniken
Mary Caroline Brandeburg Stoutenmyer		Nov 18, 1810	dau of Mr & Mrs Mat Stoutenmyer
Patrick Garick		Nov 18, 1810	son of John & Catherine Garick
John Martin Brandeburg		Nov 25, 1810	son of John & Rosina Brandeburg
Shadrack Brandeburg		Dec 9, 1810	son of Adam & Sophia Brandeburg
Morgan Irick		Dec 11, 1810	son of Valentine & Mary Irick
David Barbour		Jan 13, 1811	son of Mr & Mrs George Barbour
Elisabeth Margaret Gates		Jan 27, 1811	dau of Christian & Magdelen Gates
James Ludwig Hair		Feb 24, 1811	son of James & Margaret Hair
George Alexander Ziegler		Feb 24, 1811	son of George & Rachell Ziegler
Elisabeth Keller		Apr 7, 1811	dau of Mr & Mrs Philip Keller
William Gates		Apr 21, 1811	son of Frederick & Rosina Gates
Anne Susanna Rast		Apr 21, 1811	dau of Mr & Mrs Conrad Rast

Childrens Names	When Born	When Christened	Parents Names
Eve Mary Holman	Apr 6, 1811	May 12, 1811	dau of John Conrad & Rachell Holman
John Henry Stiffelmyer		May 19, 1811	son of Elisabeth Stiffelmyer
Anne Eliza Garick		June 30, 1811	dau of William & Anne Garick
Robert Crabb Gilbert		July 7, 1811	son of Mr David & Catherine Gilbert
Anne Parler		Aug 10, 1811	dau of Mr & Mrs Abednego Parler
John Cummings		Sep 1, 1811	son of Mr & Mrs Cummings
Catherine Cummings		Sep 1, 1811	dau of Mr & Mrs Cummings
James Joseph Stoutenmyer		Sep 12, 1811	son of Mr & Mrs Mathias Stoutenmyer
William Mintz		Sep 29, 1811	son of Mr & Mrs Frederick Mintz
Alexander Brandeburg		Sep 29, 1811	son of Martin & Catherine Brandeburg
Jacob Ziegler		Oct 27, 1811	son of Jacob & Margaret Ziegler
Mary Sellers		Oct 27, 1811	dau of Mr & Mrs Andrew Sellers
Christopher Cubstead		Nov 15, 1811	son of Mr & Mrs Cubstead
Eleanora Louisa Haigler		Nov 17, 1811	dau of Mr & Mrs Henry Haigler
Jennet de Bardaleben	Jan 8, 1812	Jan 31, 1812	dau of Arthur & Mary Bardaleben
John Joseph Stider		Jan 31, 1812	son of Mr & Mrs John Stider
----- Felkle		Feb 7, 1812	son of Mr & Mrs Melchior Felkle
Anne Harriet	Jan --, 1812	Feb 9, 1812	dau of Mr & Mrs Daniel Fogel
Anne Rebecca Hoffman	Dec 26, 1811	Feb 23, 1812	dau of Mr & Mrs John & Mary Hoffman
Martha Hiller		Apr 18, 1812	dau of Mr & Mrs Hiller, Dutch Fork
Mary Anne Gabel		Apr 19, 1812	dau of Mr & Mrs Gabel, Dutch Fork
Mary Burkett		July 1, 1812	dau of Mr & Mrs Casper Burkett
Anne Elisabeth Garick		July 5, 1812	dau of John & Catherine Garick
Charlotte Sarah Fisher		July 16, 1812	dau of John & Charlotte Fisher
Anne Weissenhand		Sep 27, 1812	dau of George & Catherine Weissenhand
Elisa Frederica Menniken		Oct 1, 1812	dau of John & Elisabeth Menniken
Joshua Myers		Oct 4, 1812	son of David & Elisabeth Myers
Charlotte Fogel		Oct 8, 1812	dau of John & Magdelen Fogel
----- Irick		Oct 11, 1812	son of Valentine & Mary Irick
----- Garick		--- 11, 1812	son of George & Magdelen Garick
Maddison Goodwin)		--- 21, 1812	son & dau of Mr Goodman, Guilford Co., NC
Ann Elisa Goodwin)		--- 21, 1812	dau of General Gray, Guilford Co., NC
Mary Gray			
Jacob Edmond Hair		Nov 8, 1812	son of James & Magdelen Hair
David Martin) Stoutenmyer twins		Nov 8, 1812	son & dau of Mr & Mrs Daniel Stoutenmyer
Anne Elisa)			
Jacob Ziegler		--- 12, 1812	son of George & Rachell Ziegler
Mary Eugenia Brandeburg		--- 22, 1812	dau of Adam & Sophia Brandeburg

12

Childrens Names	When Born	When Christened	Parents Names
Eleanora Eugenia Gates	Nov 23, 1812	Dec 17, 1812	dau of Frederick & Rosina Gates
Elina Rebecca Myers		--- 21, 1812	dau of Mr & Mrs Myers, Sandy Run, SD
David Ranch		--- 29, 1812	son of George Steven Ranch
Catherine Susanna Houser		--- 30, 1812	dau of Jacob & Elisabeth Houser
Sarah Anne Erwin	Nov 1, 1812	Jan 5, 1813	dau of James David & Sarah Frances Erwin
John Christian Gates		--- 10, 1813	son of Christian & Magdalen Gates
Jacob Henry Hair		Mar 7, 1813	son of James & Margaret Hair
Mary Margaret Garick		--- 7, 1813	dau of Mr & Mrs William Garick
Godfrey Gates		--- 22, 1813	son of Mr & Mrs John Gates, Beaver Creek
Mary Cobel		Apr 5, 1813	dau of Mr & Mrs Cobel at Salketcher
Rebecca Sellers		--- 16, 1813	dau of William & Elisabeth Sellers
William Charles Gray		--- 18, 1813	son of Stephen & Elisabeth Grey
Joseph Hoffman		May 2, 1813	son of Mr & Mrs Hoffman, Dutch Fork
John Russell Holman		--- 9, 1813	son of John Conrad & Rachell Holman
James Russell Gates		--- 9, 1813	son of Conrad & Elisabeth Gates
John Keller	Apr 7, 1813	July 28, 1813	son of Philip & Margaret Keller
Mary Kegler)			
Anne Kegler)		July 28, 1813	daus of Mr & Mrs John Kegler, Dargate
Elisabeth Inneger		Aug 12, 1813	dau of Mr & Mrs Inneger, Dutch Fork
Eugenia Ray		Sep 5, 1813	dau of John & Magdelen Raye
Eleanora Eugenia Hoffman	Apr 16, 1813	Sep 12, 1813	dau of Barbara Hoffman
Catherine Carolina Haigler		Sep 26, 1813	dau of Rosina & A. Haigler
Jesse Nuel Haigler		Oct 10, 1813	son of Mr & Mrs HY Haigler
John Andrew Ziegler		Oct 30, 1813	son of Mr & Mrs Jacob Ziegler
Catherine Carolina Keller		Nov 14, 1813	dau of John & Mary Keller
Mary Magdelen Rast		Nov 14, 1813	dau of Mr & Mrs Conrad Rast
Eugenia Stoutemyer		Dec 4, 1813	dau of Mr & Mrs Mat Stoutenmyer
Mary Ann Ryser		Dec 16, 1813	dau of Mr & Mrs Josiah Ryser

The following was entered in the original in a different handwriting: (At bottom of page)

James Thomas Holman	Oct 23, 1814	Nov 15, 1815	son of John Conrad & Rachel Holman
Elizabeth Rachel Holman	Dec 8, 1817		dau of Jn C. & Rachel Holman
Jesse Knodle Holman	Nov 7, 1818		son of Jn C. & Rachel Holman
Ann Catherine Holman	Jan 22, 1821		dau of Jn C. & Rachel Holman
John Joseph Holman	Oct 9, 1823		son of Jn C. & Rachel Holman
Eugenia Rebaca Holman	Feb 11, 1826		dau of Jn C. & Rachell Holman
David Luther Holman	June 16, 1829		son of Jn C. & Rachel Holman

*All the preceeding Baptisms were by Rev. Franklow

A memorandum of children baptized since the consecration of the new church, St. Matthew's:
Also, their ages, when baptized and the names of their parents - Here are also the ages of some that
were baptized in the old church before the consecration of the new church.

Childrens Names	When Born	When Baptized	Parents Names
David Bowl Karrick	May 22, 1827		son of William Karrick & Nancy Snyder
Mary Magdalene Karrick	Apr 15, 1828		dau of Daniel Karrick & Barbara Brandeburg
Mary Katherine Rast	Nov 27, 1827		dau of John A. Rast & Mary Charlotte Haigler
James Manning Irick	Oct 3, 1827	Dec 16, 1827	son of John A. Irick & Rebecca Ann Parlour
James Alexander Bookhart			son of John Nicholas Bookhart & Eliz. Entzminger
Jane Elizabeth Bookhart			dau of John N. Bookhart & Elizabeth Entzminger
Charles Richardson Irick	Mar 9, 1826		son of John Martin Irick & Eliza Killingsworth
John Calvin Harman	Sep 1, 1826		son of Jacob Harman & Mary Felkle
Katherine Harman	Oct 14, 1821		dau of Jacob Harman & Mary Felkle
John David Rast	Feb 3, 1826	Mar 16, 1826	son of John A. Rast & Charlotte Haigler
Peter Edward)	Jan 29, 1828	Mar 2, 1828	son & dau of John Wiles & Elizabeth Slaughtemyer
Ugenia Katherine Wiles) twins			
Ann E.C. Huffman	Feb 12, 1825	Mar 5, 1825	dau of Daniel Huffman & K. Huffman
Susan Elizabeth Huffman	Jan 4, 1827	Feb 13, 1827	dau of Daniel Huffman & K. Huffman
James Russell Gates	Apr 5, 1827	May 1 Sunday	son of Lewis L. Gates & Ann Sloughtemyer
John McGrill	Mar 15, 1816		son of John McGrill & Charlotte Gates
Richard Alexander McGrill	Dec 15, 1818		son of John McGrill & Charlotte Gates
Samuel D. McGrill	Apr 23, 1823		son of John McGrill & Charlotte Gates
Eliza Elenor McGrill	May 10, 1825		dau of John McGrill & Charlotte Gates
George David Gates	Sep 21, 1827		son of Wm. Gates & Eve Stifflemyer
John Martin Karick	Sep 29, 1812		son of Wm. Karick & Nancy Snyder
Mary Elizabeth Karick	Mar 30, 1815		dau of Wm. Karick & Nancy Snyder
George Wm. Karick	Feb 12, 1818		son of Wm. Karick & Nancy Snyder
Daniel Joseph Karick	Nov 28, 1820		son of Wm. Karick & Nancy Snyder
Charles David Karick	Jan 24, 1824		son of Wm. Karick & Nancy Snyder
Derril Shadrick Karick	Nov 3, 1827		son of Wm. Karick & Nancy Snyder
Elizabeth Margaret Irick	Dec 31, 1821		dau of Martin Irick & Eliza Irick
William Martin Irick	Jan 2, 1824		son of Martin Irick & Eliza Irick

BURIALS - 1836
D. Bernhard - Pastor

1836

Jan 12th	Mrs. Rast
Jan 14th	Phillip King
Apr 22nd	Mrs. Ulmer
June 8th	Joseph Keller
July 15th	Mr. Hairs child
July 22nd	N. Bookhards child
July 24th	N. Stromans child
Aug 11th	A. Rasts child
Aug 19th	John J. Keller
Oct 25th	Mrs. Kitts child
Oct 30th	Mr. Caricks child
Nov 18th	Mr. Caler
Dec 11th	Frederick Wolf
Dec 24th	Mrs. Rast

1837

Jan 2nd	John C. Holman
Jan 8th	Mary Wissenhunt
Jan 20th	James T. Holman
Jan 22nd	Rachel Holman
Jan 23rd	Wm. C. Holman
Feb 10th	Geo. Rast

The following is a list of the members of St. Matthew's Lutheran Church as taken on the 27th January 1839 all of whom do solemnly pledge themselves to be governed by the Formula and discipline of the Lutheran Church as drawn up by said church in Convention assembled and ratified by Synod Nov. 14th 1838. D. Bernhard, Pastor of St. Matthew's Church.

1. Christian Cates (dead)
2. John H. Haigler (died)
3. John Bookhardt (dead)
4. John N. Bookhardt
5. David McClure
6. John M. Irick
7. Adam Rast (died)
8. Wm. Karick
9. Peter Fogle
10. John L. Haigler
11. James Haigler
12. Jesse N. Haigler
13. Patrick Haigler
14. George Haigler
15. Jacob Keller (dead)
16. Charles Stoudenmire
17. Charles Austin (died)
18. Nicholas Stroman
19. Daniel Huffman
20. Adam Karick (jun)
21. John W. Keller
22. James Barber
23. Jacob Harman
24. Martin Karick
25. Catherine Haigler (dead)
26. Catharine Keller
27. Jane Austin (dead)
28. Rachel Calor (dead)
29. Eugena Wannamaker
30. Elizabeth Wannamaker
31. Mary Hair
32. Elizabeth Zimmerman
33. Mary Jackson
34. Rosanna Jackson
35. Mary Ann Jackson (Thier)
36. Susannah Keller
37. Mary Irick (dead)
38. Mary Huffman
39. Mary Roiser
40. Rosanna Cates
41. Christena Fersner
42. Mary Bookhardt
43. Eliza Irick
44. Elizabeth Fogle
45. Elizabeth Bookhardt
46. Polly Cates

47. Mary Hungepeler
48. Louisa Hungerpeler (Method)
49. Elizabeth Hungerpeler
50. Mary B. Haigler
51. Elizabeth S. Haigler (dead)
52. Margaret Haigler
53. Mary Harman
54. Catherine Harman (Wissenhunt)
55. Mary Ann Fogle
56. Magdalen Keller
57. Charlotte L. Cates
58. Julia Ann Irick
59. Ann E. Watt
60. Catherine Wolf
61. Eliza Rast (died)
62. Charlotte Rast
63. Eugena Mack
64. Harriet R. Wiles
65. Mary McClure
66. Mary B. Huffman
67. Elizabeth Snider
68. Mary Snider (Dantzler-Methodist)
69. Sophia Kerrick
70. Elizabeth Burket
71. Ann Burket
72. Louisa (N.?) Stroman
73. Ann Haigler
74. Sarah M. Haigler
75. Rachel Keller
76. Mary T. Irick
77. Mary Stroudenmire
78. Charlotte Stoudenmire (moved away)
79. Caroline Karick
80. Catherine Karick
81. Ann Jane Haigler
82. Rosanna Huffman
83. Ann Karick
84. Elizabeth Haigler (died)
85. Adam Burket
86. Lewis Burket
87. Rebecca Stone
88. Elizabeth Burket
89. Margaret Stone
90. Elizabeth A. Fersner
91. Charlotte McGrill
92. Barbara Stoudenmire
93. Margaret Hair
94. Adam Haigler (dead)
95. Samuel Hubler (Methodist)
96. John Haigler
97. John Peter Haigler
98. Mary Stoudenmire
99. Mary Dardes Vise
100. Elizabeth Mineger (moved in fork)
101. Elizabeth Ross
102. Mary Ann Irick
103. Margaret Carick
104. Elizabeth Carick
105. Wm. Watts
106. Elizabeth Shirlnight
107. Henry Houk
108. Valentine Irick
109. Henry A. Haigler
110. Ellen Keller
111. Mary Rast (died)
112. Ellen Huffman
113. Elisabeth Parler
114. Elizabeth Irick
115. Margaret Smoke
116. Ann Smoke
117. Ann Houck
118. Eugena Gates
119. Rossanna Parler
120. Sarah Riser
121. Mary Stone
122. Jeremiah Gates
123. Joshua Haigler

The following is a list of the Members of St.Matthew's Congregation at the time of the organization of Mt. Lebanon, also of those who have been received since that time. Mount Lebanon congregation was organized on the 13th day of Jan. 1844. J.P. Margart, Pastor.

1. Christian Gates (dead)
2. John Bookhardt (dead)
3. J.N. Bookhardt (Pinegrove)
4. D.C. McClure (Pinegrove)
5. J.M. Irick Sen (dead)
6. William Garick (Pine Grove
7. Peter Fogle (deceased)
8. N. Patrick Haigler (dec.)
9. Charles Stoudenmyer (Pinegr)
10. Daniel Huffman (removed)
11. Adam Garick Jun. (Pinegr.)
12. John W. Keller (removed)
13. James Barber (dead)
14. Jacob Harmon (dead)
15. Martin Garick (removed)
16. Catherine Keller (dead)
17. Jane Austin (dead)
18. Eugenia Carr (dead)
19. Elizabeth Wannamaker (Pngr.)
20. Mary Hair (Pinegrove)
21. Elizabeth Zimmerman (dead)
22. Mary jackson (Pinegrove)
23. Rosanna Jackson (Pinegrove)
24. Mary Ann Shirer (Pinegrove)
25. Susanah Keller (removed)
26. Mary Huffman (removed)
27. Mary Riser (Pinegrove)
28. Rosanna Gates (dead)
29. Mary Bookhardt (Pinegrove)
30. Eliza Irick (dead)
31. Elizabeth Fogle (Pinegrove)
32. Elizabeth Bookhardt (Pngr)
33. Polly Gates (dead)
34. Mary Hungerpeler (Meth?)
35. Elizabeth Hungerpealer
36. Mary Harmon (dead)
37. Catherine Wissenhunt (died)
38. Mary Ann Zeagler (Pngrove)
39. Charlotte L. Gates (dead)
40. Mary Julia Ann Gates
41. Ann E. Watt (Pinegrove)
42. Mary Charlotte Rast
43. Eugenia Mack (Pinegrove)
44. Mary McClure (Pinegrove)
45. Mary B. Huffman (removed)
46. Elizabeth Snyder
47. Sophia Garick (Pinegrove)
48. Elisabeth Burket (Pngrove)
49. Ann Burket (deceased)
50. Rachel Keller (removed)
51. Mary Stoudenmeyer (dead)
52. Caroline Weils (removed)
53. Catharine Garick (Pinegrove)
54. Ann Jane Haigler
55. Rosanna Huffman (removed)
56. Elizabeth S. Haigler
57. Adam Burkett (Pinegrove)
58. Lewis Burkett (Pinegrove)
59. Rebecca Stone (removed)
60. Margaret Stone (removed)
61. Charlotte McGrill (Pinegrove)
62. Margaret Hair (Pinegrove)
63. John Haigler (dead)
64. Mary Stoudenmeyer (Pinegrove)
65. Mary Dorcas Vise (Pinegrove)
66. Elizabeth Ross (Pinegrove)
67. Mary Irick (dead)
68. Margaret Garick (Pinegrove)
69. Lewis Huffman
70. Wm. Watt (dead)
71. Henry A. Haigler (dead)
72. Ellen Wolfe (dead)
73. Ellen Garick (removed)
74. Elizabeth Parler (removed)
75. Elizabeth Irick (dead)
76. Margaret Smoke (Dufford-Pngr)
77. Ann Smoke (Pinegrove)
78. Ann Houck (Bair-Methodist)
79. Eugenia Myers (removed)
80. Sarah Riser (Strock-removed)
81. Jeremiah Gates (dead)
82. Susannah Huffman (removed)
83. Frances Rast (Keller)
84. Sarah Austin (Burke-removed)
85. Caroline Austin (Clemons-rem)
86. John Mack (Pinegrove)
87. Mary Shirer (dead)
88. Eliza Fogle (Zeagler-Pngrove)
89. Ann Houser (Pinegrove)
90. S. Thos. Hendric (deceased)
91. Ann C. Hendric (removed)
92. Russel Hungerpealer (dead)
93. John Hungerpealer (dead)
94. John David Rast (deceased)
95. Henry Garick (removed)
96. David B. Garick
97. Jos. Garick (Pinegrove)
98. George Garick (Pinegrove)
99. Jos. G. Zeagler (Pinegrove)
100. A.G. Zeagler (Pinegrove)

NOTE - In the interest of space, some abbreviations have been used. Ex. - Pngr. - Pinegrove; Meth. - Methodist; rem. - removed

Members of St. Matthew's Congregation - Jan 13, 1844, cont'd.

101. Christian Gates (dead)
102. Adam Shirer (Pinegrove)
103. Jacob Keller (deceased)
104. David Stoudenmeyer
105. Ann Shirer (Houser-Pngr)
106. Jane Bookhard (Way-dead)
107. Mary Parler (dead)
108. Ann Watt
109. Mary Ann Irick (Bradum)
110. Maria Keller (dead)
111. Ann Carr (Pinegrove)
112. Mary Ann Weeks (dead)
113. Mary Huffman (removed)
114. Adeline Brandeburg (dead)
115. David Smoke (excl.)
116. Rebecca Smoke (deceased)
117. Eliza McGrill (Pinegrove)
118. Aaron Gates (dead)
119. Aaron Keller (removed)
120. James Weils
121. Lewis Hungerpealer (dead)
122. Samuel Johnson (removed)
123. Emanuel Fogle (Pinegrove)
124. Lewis Keller (Pinegrove)
125. Sarah Jackson (removed)
126. John Riser (Pinegrove)
127. Joseph Riser (removed)
128. Margaret Rast
129. Charles Colsey (removed)
130. David Fogle (Pinegrove)
131. Scheck Hungerpieler (dead)
132. Schwartz Hungerpieler
133. Wm. Houck (dead)
134. Ann Hoover (removed)
135. Eliza Hoover (removed)
136. Russel H. Zimmerman
137. George D. Rast
138. Mary Hungerpieler Jun (Meth)
139. Selena Huffman (removed)
140. Martha C. Barber (dead)
141. Jane McClure (Pinegrove)
142. Emanual Wiles
143. Joseph A. Keller
144. Mary M. Haigler (dead)
145. Lovey Keller (removed)
146. Jane Keller (removed)
147. Melchoir Huffman (removed)
148. James Felkel (deceased)
149. Russel Keller (dead)
150. Sarah Haigler (dead)
151. Lawrence Bradham (dead)
152. Derril Felkel (excluded)
153. John Felkel
154. George Wissenhunt (dead)
155. Barba E. Gates (by certif)
156. Robert Irick, Junr. (Pngr.)

NOTE: - In the interest of space, several abbreviations have been used. by certif - by certificate; Pngr. - Pinegrove.

The following is a list of the members of St. Matthew's Church taken Nov 3rd 1853.

1. J.M. Irick (dead)
2. Jamy Barber (dead)
3. Jacob Harmon (dead)
4. Martin Garick (removed)
5. Catherine Keller (removed)
6. Ugenia Carr (dead)
7. Elisabeth Zimmerman (dead)
8. Rossanna Gates (deceased)
9. Elisa Irick (dead)
10. Polly Gates (dead)
11. Mary Hungerpeiler (dead)
12. Elisabeth Hungerpieler
13. Mary Harmon (dead)
14. Catherine Wissenhunt (dec)
15. C. Louisa Gates (dead)
16. M. Julia Ann Gates (dead)
17. Ann E. Watt (Pinegrove)
18. M. Charlotte Rast (dec)
19. Elizabeth Snider (Trinity)
20. Mary Stoudenmire
21. Ann Jane Haigler
22. Elizabeth S. Haigler (dead)
23. Elisabeth Garick Huffman (removed)
24. William Watt (Pinegrove)
25. Henry A. Haigler (deceased)
26. Ellen Wolfe (Methodist)
27. Elisabeth Irick (Pinegrove)
28. Jeremiah Gates (dead)
29. Francy Keller
30. Russel Hungerpieler, Pr., dec
31. Christian Gates (deceased)
32. David Stoudenmire (dead)
33. Mary Ann Bradham (Baptist)
34. Mary Ann Weeks (Felder-Pngr)
35. Adeline Brandenburg (removed)
36. Aaron Gates (deceased)
37. Lewis Hungerpieler (dead)
38. Margaret Rast (removed)
39. Henry Carr (dead)
40. Sheck Hungerpieler (dead)
41. Schwartz Hungerpieler
42. William Houck (Preacher)
43. Russel Zimmerman
44. Mary M. Haigler (Houck)
45. George D. Rast
46. Martha C. Barber (Houck)

List of members Nov 3, cont'd.

47. Emanuel Wiles (Houck)
48. Dr. J.A. Keller (expelled)
49. Russel Keller (expelled)
50. Sarah Haigler (Bull) (exp)
51. Lawrence Bradham (Bapt.)
52. Robert Irick Jun (Trinity)
53. John Felkel (removed)
54. Dr. M.K. Holman
55. Adriana Haigler (removed)
56. James Rast
57. Barbara E. Gates (Jackson)
58. Lewis Huffman (deceased)
59. David Eades (deceased)
60. Jefferson Gates (dead)
61. Frederick Gates
62. J---? Harmon Junr (dead)
63. Mary Ann Wisenhunt (Felkel)
64. Rachel Eades
65. Henry E. Haigler (removed)

Adriana Zimmerman (Tilley)
Wm. E. Barber
Anna A. Zimmerman
Olivia Gates
Martha C. Wolfe
Henrietta C. Barber (removed)
Mary Della Keller (dead)
Frances M. Wissenhunt (Methodist)
Dr. J.A. Keller (dismissed)
Anna Rast
Ellison Gates
Martha Haigler (certificate)
Mary Ann Eades (expelled)
George Gates (expelled)
Georgiana Haigler (certificate)
Thomas Stellinger (dropped)
Sarah Stellinger (dropped)
Alice Barber
John C. Harman
Margaret A. Holman
Emma Holman

On the bottom of this sheet is written:
I forgot David Eades & the little Gateses. When I and Jesse compared lists I found more to put down.

List of Members of St. Matthew's Church revised Jan 9th, 1867.

1. J.M. Irick (dead)
2. J.W. Barber (dead)
3. Jacob Harman (dead)
4. Catharine Keller
5. Elizabeth Zimmerman
6. Polly Gates (dead)
7. Elizabeth Hungerpeler (dec)
8. Mary Harman (dead)
9. Catherine Wissenhunt
10. C. Louisa Gates (dead)
11. M. Julia Ann Gates
12. Ann Jane Haigler
13. Frances Keller
14. R.H. Zimmerman
15. Mary M. Houck

16. G.D. Rast
17. Martha C. Barber
18. Emanuel Wiles (dead)
19. W.R. Keller
20. Sarah Bull
21. Dr. M.K. Holman
22. Adriana Stoudenmire
23. J.L. Rast
24. Barbera E. Jackson (dead)
25. David Eades (dead)
26. F.I. Gates
27. Mary Ann Felkel
28. Rachel Eades
29. Adriana Sellers

Members Received by Rev. Derrick

30. W.E. Barber
31. Anna R. Zimmerman
32. Olivia Gates
33. Martha C. Wolfe
34. Harriet C. Barber
35. Frances M. Arant (removed)
36. Anna Rast
37. Ellison Gates
38. Martha Haigler (removed)
39. Georgiana Haigler (removed)
40. Sarah Stillinger (removed)
41. Alice Barber
42. John C. Harman
43. Margaret A. Holman

44. Emma Holman
45. George Gates (dead)
46. C.E. Birchmore
47. Mary Ellen Gates (dead)
48. Martha E. Keller
49. Alice M. Gates (dead)
50. Ann Keller
51. Elizabeth E. Keller
52. Eliza C. Brandenburg
53. Jefferson M. Keller (dism.)
54. Bachman W. Gates
55. Ida C. Keller
56. Fanny C. Felkel
57. Emma J. Felkel (dead)

List of Members revised Jan 9th, 1867, cont'd.

58. David Absolum Walling	62. Mary Eve Barber
59. Corrie Holman	63. Catherine Wiles
60. Aron Barber	64. Eugene Barber
61. Joseph K. Felkel	65. James Barber
	66. Annie Rast

G.A. Hough, 1873

Members by Rev. T. Hawkins

We find no list of members reaching the ministery of Rev. Hallman & Wilson. The following have been rec'd by T. Hawkins.

Capt. J.W. Sellers
Jas. M. Holman
Pearl Parlor
Miss Effie Brandenburgh
Miss Connie Brandenburgh
Wesley Wiles
Mrs. W. Wiles
Mary Jane Holman)
George Holman)   children of Dr. M.K.H.
Mary Haigler (Frank's dau.)
Willie Oliver
Ada Oliver
Jesse Layton
Jas. R. Brandenburg
John K. Brandenburg
Jas. W. Brandenburg
Harry C. Brandenburg
Minnie A. Brandenburg
Willie Rush)
Willie Rast) 1892
John Gates, Sept.? 15, 1892, Fort Motte

Baptisms During the Pastorate of the Rev. Paul Derrick

Childrens Names	When Born	When Christened	Parents Names
Rosa Christianna		June 19, 1859	dau of R.W. & Ann Keller
Adrianna Sellers		Sep 15, 1860	dau of J.W. & M.C. Barber
Jacob Patrick		Nov 11, 1860	son of Rev. W.A. & M. Houck
Thomas Milton		Feb 24, 1861	son of J.A. & Rosa Felkel
George Edward		May 12, 1862	son of J.L. & Anna Rast
Margaret Ann		Aug 17, 1862	dau of G.D. & M.J. Rast
Anna Josephine		Oct 6, 1863	dau of J.K & M.A. Felkel
William Derrick		Oct 28, 1862	son of Rev. W.A. & M. Houck
Thomas Francis Marion		June 26, 1864	son of Thomas & S. Stillinger
Catherine Elizabeth		Mar 11, 1865	dau of J.K. & M.A. Felkel
Martha Jane Eliza		May 13, 1865	dau of Thomas & S. Stillinger
Claudius Judson		Aug 26, 1865	son of J.L. & Anna Rast
John David		Dec 27, 1866	son of Davis & R. Edes
John James David)		Dec 27, 1866	children of T. Stillinger
Elizabeth Henrietta)		Dec 27, 1866	
Martha Shingler		Dec 30, 1866	dau of J.W. & M.C. Barber
James Moss		Aug 28, 1868	son of M.K. & Emma Holman
Jacob David		Apr 25, 1868	son of J.K. & M.A. Felkel
Novice Delura		June 14, 1868	dau of J.L. & Anna Rast
Jefferson A. Dantzler		Nov 16, 1868	son of F.I. & Mary E. Gates
George Adam	Jan 1, 1869	Feb 28, 1869	son of G.D. & M.J. Rast
Wilber Leonidas Houck		Feb 28, 1869	son of W.D. & Carrie Riser
Charles William Jacob	Jan 1, 1869	July 25, 1869	son of C.E. & Christiana Birchmore
Ann Caroline	Jan 1, 1869	Aug 15, 1869	dau of Dr. M.K. & E. Holman
Frederick Mortimer	Jan 1, 1870	Mar 20, 1870	son of F.I. & M.E. Gates
Effe Gertrude		Nov 9, 1870	dau of T. Perry & Eliza Brandenburg
Adline Charlotte		Nov 9, 1870	dau of T. Perry & Eliza Brandenburg
James Russel			son of John & M.E. Brandenburg
Mary Augusta	May 3, 1871	July 20, 1871	dau of Frederick I. & Mary Ella Gates

Baptisms during the Pastorate of the Rev. J.P. Margart

Childrens Names	When Born	When Baptised	Parents Names
Ann Rebecca	Sep 2, 1840	May 9, 1841	dau of S.B. & Ann E. Parlor
Frances Emeline	Mar 17, 1841	May 9, 1841	dau of J.N. & Elizabeth Bookhart
Mary Elizabeth Ann	Apr 19, 1841	May 23, 1841	dau of Derrill & Ann Houser
Mary Jane	June 25, 1841	Aug 1, 1841	dau of John & Eugenia Mack
Martha Rebecca	Apr --, 1841	Aug 8, 1841	dau of Lewis & Elizabeth Burkett
Mary Ann Catherine	Aug 6, 1841	Oct 10, 1841	dau of David J. & Catherine Wissinhunt
Edwina Maria	July 29, 1841	Oct 10, 1841	dau of John M. & Eliza Irick
Frances Irena	Sep 18, 1841	Oct 24, 1841	dau of William & Elizabeth Watt
Nancy Eugenia	Oct 8, 1841	Nov 14, 1841	dau of Charles & S.B. Stoudenmyer
		Nov 21, 1841	dau of David & Elizabeth Fersner
Edinborough Flowers	Nov 26, 1841	Feb 13, 1842	dau of W.R. & Catherine Irick
William David	Dec 11, 1841	Feb 13, 1842	son of John A. & Mary Ann Shirer
Ann Mary Julia	Jan 7, 1842	Apr 16, 1842	dau of J.P. & A.C. Margart
Ann Rebecca		Aug 7, 1842	dau of Adam & Mary Burkett
Adam Gideon	June 21, 1842	Aug 21, 1842	son of Adam & Catherine Garick
William Lewis	Aug --, 1842	Sep 25, 1842	son of John L. & Mary B. Haigler
Joseph Albert		Oct 23, 1842	son of Samuel & Mary Rast
Luther Whitfield	Oct 12, 1842	Nov 20, 1842	son of George R. & Margaret Haigler
Francis Marion	Nov 15, 1842	Dec 18, 1842	son of Jesse N. & Caroline Haigler
Mary Ann Eliza		Jan 8, 1843	dau of David & Mary Stoudenmyer
John David Friendly		Jan 8, 1843	son of George & M. Dorcas Vise
Mary Eliza Josephine		Jan 22, 1843	dau of S.B. & Elizabeth Parlor
Lewis Shadrach) twins	Aug 4, 1842	Feb 19, 1843	sons of David & Catharine Barber
John Thomas)			
John Lewis		Mar 19, 1843	son of J.W. & Rachel Keller
Cornelia Eliza		Apr 7, 1843	dau of David & Elizabeth Fersner
Adriana Christina	Mar 6, 1843	Apr 23, 1843	dau of N.P. & Elizabeth Haigler
Julia Eugena		May 28, 1843	dau of Joseph & Christina Fersner
Harriet Eliza	May 5, 1843	June 5, 1843	dau of John & Eugena Mack
Luther Edward		July 2, 1843	son of Daniel & Rosanna Huffman
Russel Daniel	Sep 14, 1842	Sep 8, 1843	son of Russel & Elizabeth Zimmerman
Joel Franklin	Oct 8, 1843	Oct 31, 1843	son of John N. & Elizabeth Bookhart
Franklin Stookecher	May 4, 1843	Nov 12, 1843	son of John P. & A.C. Margart
Ellison Wm Lewis		Feb 18, 1844	son of George & Louisa Gates
Samuel DAniel Manders	Aug 25, 1843	Feb 18, 1844	son of Samuel & Mary Rast

Baptisms during the Pastorate of the Rev. J.P. Margart, cont'd.

Childrens Names	When Born	When Baptised	Parents Names
Jane Elizabeth	Apr 26, 1844	June 7, 1844	dau of A.J. & Elizabeth Shurlough
James Peter	Jan 31, 1844	June 30, 1844	son of Henry & Mary Garick
William Edward	June 13, 1844	July 28, 1844	son of James W. & Martha C. Barber

Baptisms by the Rev. Derrick

Rosa Christina	June 19, 1859	dau of R.W. & Ann Keller
Adriana Sellers	Sep 15, 1860	dau of J.W. & Martha Barber
Jacob Patrick	Nov 11, 1860	son of Rev. W. & Mary Houck
George Edward	May 12, 1862	son of J.L. & Anna Rast
Margaret Ann	Aug 17, 1862	dau of G.D. & Mary Jane Rast
Wm. Derrick	Oct 28, 1863	son of Rev. W. & Mary Houck
Claudius Judson	Aug 26, 1866	son of J.L. & Anna Rast

Baptisms during the Pastorate of the Rev. Geo. R. Haigler

Joel Adams	June 1848	son of George & Elizabeth Irick
Ann Amelia	July 1848	dau of David & Elizabeth Fersner
---- -----	Sep 1848	dau of Rev. Kistler & wife
John C. Calhoun	Mar 10, 1849	son of Joseph & Christina Felkel
Alice Elizabeth	Sep 16, 1849	dau of Jamy & Martha Barber
John Peter	Sep 29, 1849	son of Jesse & Caroline Haigler
Georgiana	Nov 4, 1849	dau of Patrick & Elizabeth Haigler
George F. Gusbern (?)	by E. Dufford	son of George & Margaret Haigler
Clarence Hoover	Dec 30, 1850	son of Lewis & Mary Haigler
William Henry	Dec 1850	son of Lawrence & Mary Bradham

Rev. Derricks Pastorate

Childrens Names		When Born	When Baptised	Parents Names
Christina Keller		Houck	1859	dau of Rupel Keller
Samuel Houck Derrick	by Rev.	Derrick		son of Rev. P. Derrick
Adriana Tilly				dau of James W. Barber
Jacob Patrick	by Rev.		Nov 11, 1860	son of Rev. Houck & wife
Adam Osgood)	by Rev.	Derrick	Mar 9, 1861	twin sons of A.O. & E. Holman
M. Kennerly)			Aug 31, 1861	
E. Manly Smith	by Rev.	Derrick	Aug 31, 1861	son of Jacob Smith & wife
W. Dorson	by Rev.	Derrick	May 19, 1861	son of Jacob Smith & wife
Mary Ann Eades	by Rev.	Derrick	Oct 1862	son of James & Anna Rast
George Edward Rast	by Rev.	Derrick	Oct 1862	dau of George & Mary Jane Rast
Margaret Anna Rast	by Rev.	Derrick	Nov 27, 1864	dau of E.N. & C. Haigler
Mary Agnes Haigler	by Rev.	Derrick	Aug 26, 1866	son of J.L. & Anna Rast
Claudius Judson	by Rev.	Derrick	Sep 8, 1866	son of E.N. & Carrie Haigler
Josiah Edges	by Rev.	Derrick	Dec 30, 1866	dau of J.W. & Martha Barber
Martha Shingler				

Baptisms of Negroes during the Pastorate of Rev. Geo. R. Haigler

1848

Childrens Names	Masters Names
Primus	Geo. R. Haigler
Lavina	Joshua Haigler
Joseph Mosses	Joshua Haigler
Jeremiah	Joshua Haigler

1849

Wiley	Charlotte Rast
Zebedee	H.A. Haigler
Rius	David Fersner
Amaritta	Geo. R. Haigler
Lovey	Jesse N. Haigler

1850

July 21 - Catherine	George Keitt
July 21 - Lucy	George Keitt
July 21 - John	George Keitt
July 21 - Polly	George Keitt
July 21 - Richard	George Keitt
July 21 - Hester	George Keitt
July 21 - Hiliard	George Keitt
July 21 - Sophia	Mrs. Kennerly
July 21 - Lorron	John Holman
July 21 - Sylvia	Mrs. Shuler
July 21 - Amanda	George Keitt
July 21 - Nancy	George Keitt
July 21 - Agga	George Keitt
July 21 - Ann	George Keitt
July 21 - Chloe	George Keitt
July 21 - Amelia	George Keitt
July 21 - Karianne	George Keitt
July 21 - Jane Martha	James Brandenburg
July 21 - James Noah	Mrs. E. Shuler
July 21 - Alexander Whitfield	Russel Zimmerman

Rev. T. Hawkins entered upon his duties as pastor of St. Matthew's & Mt. Lebanon Feby 10th, 1888. The new church at Mt. Lebanon was built in 1888 from funds left by James D. Keller.

No list of members is at hand. Rev. J.H. Wilson was pastor for several years and no record is found of any of his acts.

The year 1888 was noted because of the death of prominant members of this charge - R.H. Zimmerman & his wife Elisabeth, Mrs. Mary Haigler, Morgan Rast & Miss Novice Rast. No accessions except five by certificate.

                                            T. Hawkins

The year 1889 was more prosperous. Mt. Lebanon was dedicated. Rev. W.C. Shaeffer preached the sermon. Baptised on Aug 21st three children for Perry Brandenburg & five for John Brandenburg.

Elders elected at St. Matthew's - April 1st 1894

G.D. Rast   )
Dr. M.K. Holman   )   Elders
Captain J.W. Sellers)

J.L. Rast   )
F.I. Gates   )   Deacons
Harmon Rush)

Dr. Hawkins resigned at Christmas 1894 & Rev. John N. Wise was elected his successor. The salary has been $600.00 - For Rev. Wise it is $500.00

July 21st Elders elected.

St. Matthew's Church was consecrated on the 2nd of July in the year of our Lord 1826 by the Rev'd Godfrey Drehr - also on the same day the Lord's supper was administered and these are the names as follows:

George Rast...............5
Christian Gates...........3
Jn. Henry Haigler.........2
Jn. C. Holman.............2
Henry Bookhard............2
J. Adam Haigler...........1
Wm. Garick................1
Adam Rast.................2
J. Jacob Keller...........2
Lewis Haigler.............1
Charles Stoudenmire.......1
David Garick..............3
John Bookhard.............2
Jacob Keller..............2
Henry Houck...............1

Frederick Switzer..........3
Christina Felkel...........1
Conrad Rast................4
Margaret Wannamaker........1
old Mrs. Cates.............2
Margaret Haslum............1
Valentine Irick............2
John Haigler...............1
Margaret Hair..............1
Henry Switzer..............1
Barbary Hoffman............1
Rosanna Hoffman............1
Mary Switzer...............1
Elizabeth Switzer..........1

A SHORT SKETCH
OF
SAINT MATTHEW'S EV. LUTHERAN CHURCH

Orangeburg County, S.C.

Compiled from Bernheims "History of the German Settlements in the Carolinas" and other sources; by J.H.

Previous to the arrival of the first detachment of German emigrants, the only settlers occupying what is now (1889) Orangeburg county, were Henry Sterling, a trader who obtained a grant of land on Lyon's Creek and settled on it in 1704, and three or four individuals who located themselves a few years later at the Cowpens, northwest from the low country white settlements. "These" says Mills, "and the Cherokee & Catawba Indians were all the inhabitants who had preceded the Germans."

The colonists of Orangeburg county and town were mostly Germans and Swiss who came over from Europe in a large body occupying several vessels. The first colony came during the year 1735 and settled where the town of Orangeburg now stands. Another came in the following year, another in 1737, while recruits from the Fatherland continued to arrive at intervals until 1769. Besides the church in the village, one was erected a few years after the earliest arrivals in Amelia township. This latter church received the name of St. Matthews. "When it was organized" says Bernheim, who was instrumental in effecting its organization," can now only be a matter of conjecture."

From the church record book kept by Rev. John Geissendanner (the German pastor in the village of Orangeburg) and still preserved by his descendants, we learn that he often visited the German settlers in Amelia township and performed ministerial acts among them; it is im probable that he also occasionally preached there, but nothing is said concerning a church edifice and congregation having existed in Amelia township during the first years of his ministry, and there is strong reason to believe that such was not the case, in as much as he at that time connected the records of baptisms, marriages, etc. of these people with those of the Orangeburg congregation. Nevertheless as he must have labored there some nine years before any other German minister arrived, he may have been instrumental in organizing St. Matthew's Lutheran Church.

In the year 1747 Rev. Joachim Zubly, a German reform Minister removed from Frederica on St. Simons Island in Georgia on account of Spanish depredations and labored in this community. He is described by Dr. Mulenburg, who saw him on his southern tour, as an "experienced, influential, learned, prudent and very industrious man". During his ministry here Dr. Zubly organized "The German Calvinistic Church of St. John on the Four Hole", a church incorporated by the State Legislature in 1788, but now no longer in existence. This was in Orangeburg District in Amelia Township or immediately below it. Dr. Zubly afterwards removed to Savannah, Georgia.

In 1760 the Rev. John George Friederiahs, the founder of the first Lutheran church in Charleston, began to labor in Amelia township and continued here until his death, which took place either during the Revolution or immediately previous to it. Dr.

Mulenberg writes of him thus from Charleston: "I received an agreeable letter from Rev. John George Friederiahs, Luthern minister in Amelia township, one hundred miles in the country, dated October 15, 1774, in which he states that he has heard of my arrival here and was preparing for a journey to Charleston to see me but that he was prevented by sickness". I answered his letter and sought to encourage him to fight a good fight, to keep the faith, and to finish the course. He sustains a good character for sound doctrine and exemplary conduct among informed persons; he has no family, and is satisfied with the necessaries of life. A laborer standing thus alone in the wilderness among rude people, must be much encouraged when he received unexpectedly a few lines of comfort from a fellow suffering and tempted cross-bearer, as is manifest from his answer to my first letter. It is written "Woe to him that is alone".

During Rev. Friederiah's ministry here a colony of Germans came from Maine and settled in Orangeburg district, accompanied by their pastor, the Rev. Tilley. The records concerning them are scant and conflicting. J.C. Hope says, "In 1763 a colony of German Lutherans came from Maine accompanying their pastor Tilly and joined their brethren in Orangeburg district but in time, the most of these returned. Rev. Dr. Hazelius says: "Rev. Mr. Tilly arrived in South Carolina with a colony of German emigrants from Maine in the Year of 1773, but of his labors and success no accounts can be found." (An account of the German settlements in Maine may be found in "The Javelin" by Dr. Teiss, p. 170).

The Revolutionary War operated very disastrously against the German settlements & churches. As already mentioned Rev. Friederiahs died during the war or just previous to it. It is probable that St. Matthew's church was without a minister for a period of several years - from about 1775 or 1776 until 1786.

In 1788 the legislature of South Carolina incorporated fifteen German Protestant congregations "in the back part of the State of South Carolina" - among which churches is mentioned "The German Lutheran Church of St. Matthew's in Amelia Township".

In August 1786 Rev. Frederick Dasor, a young German of education who had been pastor of St. John Church in Charleston since about 1771 (regular minister part of the time and supply part) moved to Amelia Township and took charge of St. Matthew's church. Thus he was in charge when the church was incorporated. On Nov 13, 1787, a number of Lutheran and German Reformed ministers met in Zions church, Lexington District, and formed the Corpus Evangelicum or ------ Ecclesiastica in South Carolina - a sort of synodical body. Of this organization, Rev. Daser was president for several years - exactly how long cannot be determined. The "Corpus Evangelicum" seems to have met as late as 1794 or later, but the records after 1789 are so badly written and so torn that according to Dr. Hazelius, it is impossible with any degree of certainty to decipher their contents. Rev. Daser probably remained pastor of St. Matthew's until his death which took place between 1794 and 1799.

According to the evidence furnished by his book it appears that the Rev. John Philip Franklow was in charge of St. Matthew's church from 1799 till 1814. He was born in London, England in 1758 and emigrated to this country with his family, July 19, 1796 arriving in Charleston Sept. 16 of the same year. According to his own statement he was ordained and licensed to preach and baptize by the Episcopal bishop of Charleston in 1798. He was afterwards (1812) ordained and licensed by the Synod of North Carolina. This church record was begun by him and seems to have been faithfully kept as long as he remained here. In 1814 he removed to Lexington County where he remained until his death in 1829 and where many of his descendants still live (Franklows, Corleys, Hendrix, etc.). He was one of the original members of the South Carolina Synod, being present at its organization in 1824.

It is to be regretted that the ministers who followed Rev. Franklow were, none of them so careful in making a record of their official acts as he was. The History of St. Matthew's church from 1814 until 1844 is almost a blank - this book ought to contain a complete and continuing record - furnishing only meager information in disconnected scraps.

The next pastor was Rev. David Henkle, who was licensed by the North Carolina Synod in 1813. This statement is contrary to that made by Bernheim, who says "In 1814 Rev. Franklow resigned and Rev. M. Ranch became his successor". In the back part of this book however, will be found "A record of the Lutheran members of St. Matthew's Church, Amelia Township taken in part on the 4th Sunday in November 1813 and in the month of February 1814. I do hereby testify that the subscribers acknowledge that they are members of said church, consequently are under the direction of the clergy of the North Carolina convention Feb 16, 1814" Signed: " David Henkle, minister of the Gospel". It is possible that both Rev. Ranah and Henkle preached in this church at the same time. We know that Rev. Ranah preached only once a month, since he had two churches in Barnwell District and may have also preached occasionally at Sandy Run. As nearly as can now be determined, Rev. Henkle returned to North Carolina about 1815 or 1816 and Rev. Ranah remained in charge of St. Matthew's church for some years longer.

In 1822 the charge was vacant; and that year the North Carolina Synod examined and licensed Rev. Samuel Hersher, a student of Rev. Mr. Muerhoffer of Rockingham county, Virginia and sent him "to labor in the vacant congregations of Orangeburg District, South Carolina". Rev. Hersher became a member of the South Carolina Synod at its birth in 1824. In 1826 his name was "struck off", no reason being assigned for this action. His ministry here therefore appears to have ended in 1825 or 1826.

In 1826 a new church building was dedicated, July 2, by Rev. Godfrey Dreher. We do not know whether Rev. Dreher was then pastor here or not. He was pastor at one time according to Mr. Jacob F. Schirmer, and it may have been in 1826; but if so, it must have been for a short time, for the charge seems to have been vacant again in 1827; at any rate it was visited in that year by the Rev. J.D. Sheck, who was employed by the S.C. Synod to make a missionary tour through the state for the purpose of organizing churches and visiting vacant congregations. The Synods committee who read his journal and reported on it say "He labored one week at Amelia, preaching every day; he represents these people as being wealthy and respectable and possessing the largest church of any denomination in this part of the country".

There is reason to believe that Rev. Jacob Wingard preached here about this time. Mr. Schirmer says that he was once pastor of

St. Matthew's Church. It must have been between 1828 when he lived at Sandy Run and 1831 when he died. Rev. J.D. Sheck was also once pastor of this charge, though it is hard to tell precisely when. This book contains a part of a family record in which is found recorded the birth of his two children, one born July 1830 and the other in August 1831.

St. Matthew's church was also served at one time, according to Mr. Schirmer, by Rev. John C. Hope, who was ordained in 1830 and left the ministry in 1853. There is no record to tell when he preached in Orangeburg District.

Rev. Geo. Haltiwanger Sr. was licensed by the S.C. Synod in 1831, and was at some time previous to 1835 in charge of this congregation.

From 1835 to 1840 or 1841 the church was served by the Rev. David Bernhardt, a graduate of the seminary at Lexington. He was at the same time pastor of the church at Sandy Run, Lexington County.

In the latter part of 1840 or the beginning of 1841, Rev. J.P. Margart became pastor of St. Matthew's. The following article from the pen of Rev. Margart himself gives an account of some of the changes just mentioned and of the origin of Mt. Lebanon Church, and also of Pine Grove and Trinity. The article appears in the Lutheran Visitor of Apr 25, 1889 and is written to correct some error in the preceding article by Rev. W.C. Schaeff in the same paper.

COMMUNICATIONS
For the Lutheran Visitor
The Churches in Orangeburg

"Tempora Mutantur, et nos, cum illis, Mutantur".
"One generation passeth away, and another riseth up, ignorant of the facts connected with the past, except through the channels of history or tradition.

Oral tradition, however, is not always a correct channel, and in cases of discrepancy, must yield to that which is recorded.

Dear Brother Hawkins:

The above sentiments were forcibly impressed upon the mind of the undersigned by an article in THE VISITOR, over the signature of "W.C.S.", relating to the consecration of the new Mount Lebanon church, which is a part of your charge.

I do not know what gave to "W.C.S." the information he has so emphatically chronicled, for I presume he has no personal knowledge of the facts, but has written what he has heard others say. You will please permit me to state that, whoever his informant may be, the statement is incorrect so far as the history of the church and its succession of pastors is concerned. I write not from heresay but as an eye witness, and a prime actor in the premises; and can substantiate my assertion by reference to the Minutes of the S.C. Synod.

To give a true statement of the origin of Mount Lebanon church, it would be proper to go back two or three years in the history of the mother church, St. Matthew's of which the former is an off shoot.

In 1840 St. Matthew's Church was under the pastoral care of Rev. David Bernhard, of sainted memory, who for some years served that chuch and the one at Sandy Run, in Lexington county. He had associated with him, as an assistant, Rev. David Hungerpeler, a licentiate of the S.C. Synod, who also had charge of the churches on Salkehachie, in Barnwell county and Shiloh in the Fork of the Edisto in Orangeburg county. Rev. Hungerpeler died suddenly April 20th, 1840 and Rev. Bernhard applied to the Theological Seminary at Lexington, for one of the students to preach in his place. The lot fell upon the undersigned.

Rev. Bernhard finding his health declining, resigned his charge of St. Matthew's Church, and preached his farewell sermon on the last Sunday in December, 1840, retaining only the church at Sandy Run under his care.

The undersigned, having completed his theological course in November, 1840, was licensed by the S.C. Synod, at St. Paul's church, Newberry county, S.C. Being elected to succeed Rev. Bernhard in the charge of St. Matthew's church, he entered upon the duties of pastor in Jan. 1841. At that time there was a log school house at that place called Pine Grove, about five miles distant from St. Matthew's and between it and the Santee river. As there appeared to be an opening in that neighborhood for the extension of the Lutheran Church, the council of St. Matthew's agreed that their pastor should hold services at that place two

Sundays in each month. This arrangement continued year after year, and with what success, let the flourishing congregation of Pine Grove and Trinity testify.

In the course of time, it was deemed expedient to build a church in Orange parish on the Four Holes Swamp, for the accommodation of the members residing in that direction and with a view of still further extending the church. Accordingly, a building was erected, chiefly by the contribuations of the Haigler family, and being ready for service, was dedicated on Sunday, March 25th, 1843, the lamented Rev. J.F.W. Leppard assisting. The church received the name of Mount Lebanon, at the suggestion of Brother G.R. Haigler, who was then a member of the council of St. Matthews Church. At the meeting of the S.C. Synod, held at St. Matthews church, November 1843, the undersigned "proposed Brother G.R. Haigler to the ministerium for license to preach and bury the dead". Accordingly, you will find his name enrolled among the licentiates for that year. He, of course, held no charge, but acted as an assistant to the pastor, both at Mount Lebanon and at Shiloh in the Fork of the Edisto.

This arrangement continued until two meetings of the S.C. Synod held at Savannah in 1845, when Brother Haigler's liscense was "so extended as to preach the Gospel and administer the Ordinances". He then became pastor of the churches in Barnwell county and Shiloh, in the fork of Edisto, Orangeburg county, which he served for two consecutive years.

In the fall of 1847, an unpleasant circumstance occurred in the St. Matthew's pastorate, which resulted in the election of Rev. G.R. Haigler to the charge of St. Matthew's and Mount Lebanon, and the withdrawal of Pine Grove, which had till then, been a part of the charge. The undersigned then retained charge of Pine Grove church, out of which grew Trinity Church.

The foregoing statement, which can be substantiated by reference to the Minutes of the S.C. Synod, goes to prove that W.C.S. is in error when he says that Mount Lebanon was organized by Rev. G.R. Haigler, and he was their first pastor.

In giving the names of Rev. Haigler's successors, he has also made a mistake. From the year 1848 to the time of his removal to the State of Alabama, Rev. Haigler retained charge of the church composing the St. Matthew's pastorate, when he was succeeded by Rev. Paul Derrick, a very prominent member of the S.C. Synod, who has gone to his reward, but whose name W.C.S. has omitted in his list.

Permit my dear brother, in conculsion to congratulate you and the members of your charge, on the success which has attended you in the erection of so commodious and beautiful an edifice as the new Mount Lebanon church is said to be. May you and your good people continue to prosper in the future as in the past; and although the first pastor seems to have escaped the memory of some, who nearly half a century ago were babes in stature, he wishes them to know that he is still alive, and holds for them the same affectionate regard he once entertained for their ancestors, and hope they may continue to increase in spiritual and temporal prosperity, and prove themselves worthy of the bright records of the past. And though he may not be permitted to see them in the flesh nor to witness the fruits of their liberality in this life, he hopes to meet them all in a bright and happier region, where earthly records will not be needed to identify our relationship toward each other, but where we shall all see as we are seen and know as we are known.

May the peace of God that passeth all understanding abide with you forever. Amen.

Yours fraternally,

John P. Margart

CONFIRMATIONS BY THE REV. J.P. FRANKLOW

1800
Dec 21 Martin Brandeburg
George Karick
Melchior Hoffman
Elizabeth Hoffman
Barbara Koffman
Margaret Irick
Jane Stoutenmyer

1801
Ludwig Stoutenmyer
Rosina Stoutenmyer

1802
Elisabeth Burkett
John Mack
Frederick King

1803
Dec 25 John Hepworth Francklow
Martin Gates
Adam Brandeburg
Elisabeth Irick
Anne Stoutenmyer
Anne Garick

1806
May 25 Rosina Speignard
Elisabeth Irick
John Jacob Garick
William Garrick
Margaret Irick
Catherin Stoutenmyer
Sarah Frances Francklow
Elizabeth Gates

1807
Dec 25 Elisabeth de Bardeleben
Julianna de Bardeleben
Deborah Leah Franklow
Elisabeth Holman
Charlotte Gates
Anne Snider
Catherine Snider
Elizabeth Ziegler
Magdelen Hair
Catherine Rast
Mary Rast
Elizabeth Rast
Elisabeth Stiffelmyer
Mary Garick
Magdelen Switzer
Thomas Holman
Daniel Sellers
Samuel Garick
Daniel Garick

1808
Dec 25 Catherine Felkle
Mary Waltz
Martin Irick
Anne Haigler
Adam Loyd

1809
George Wissenhunt
Anne Wissenhunt
Margaret Sellers
Margaret Garick

1810
Jan 12 Sophia Garick
Sussanna Keller
Anne Keller
Margaret Switzer
Elisabeth Rast
Rosina Haigler
Margaret Rast
Jacob Felkle
John Switzer
William Rast

1811
Apr 14 Henry de Bardeleben
Samuel Kiebler
George Wise
Harriet Irick
Magdelen Brande
Catherine Meigler
Barbara Zimmerman
Mary Zimmerman

1812
Mar 29 John Buchard
Mrs. Buchard
Henry Buchard
Joseph Keller
John Slater
Mary Switzer
John Fogel
Mrs. Fogel
Daniel Fogel
George Ziegler
Mrs. Rachel Ziegler
Mrs. Elizabeth Hoffman
Mrs. Peter Hair
Adam Hair
Thomas Stiffelmyer
Thomas Slater
Elisabeth Snider
Daniel Hair
Adam Wild
Mary Weis

Confirmations by the Rev. Franklow cont'd.

1812 cont'd.
Mar 29 Daniel Stoutenmyer
        Magdelen Stoutenmyer
        Elisabeth Sellers
        George Sellers
        Mary Irick
        John Huber
        David Warne
        John Pein
        Anne Thomson
        Mary West
        Rosina Markley
        Daniel Gates
        William Wissenhunt
        Elisabeth Ryser
        Adam Brandeburg
        Sophia Brandeburg

1812
Dec 25 Andrew Hoffman
        Joseph Ryser
        Mary Ryser
        Jacob Ryser
        Ludwig Hoffman
        Sophia Hair
        Hannah Rast

1813
Jan 3   Melchoir Felkle
        John Anthony Menicken

DUTCH FORK, LEXINGTON DISTRICT S.C.

1813
June 6 David Gloeckle
        Jesse Carle
        Samuel Cark
        Ephraim Carle
        Mathias Wissenger
        Jacob Ruckett
        Jacob Gieger
        Christian Gaebel
        Daniel Kaemerlaerder
        Friederick Gaebel
        Absolom Wingart
        John Jueniger
        Valentine Gaebel
        Salome Wingart
        Anne Gloeckle
        Anne Kraemer
        Mary Leigs
        Elisabeth Luebrand
        Sarah Luebrand
        Mary Ruff
        Eve Gaebelin
        Christina Wingart
        Catherine Muetzin

1813
June 26 Daniel Zimmerman
Aug 19 Anne Walburie Garick
Dec 12 Jacob Schnider
        Daniel Neisler
        Casper Waltz
        John Felkle
        John Keller
        Magdelen Buchard
        Mary Felkle
        Rachell Holman
        Elisabeth Schnider
        Marla Irick
        Magdelen Pein
        William Gates
        Robert Shilling

CONFIRMATIONS DURING THE PASTORATE OF REV. J.P. MARGART

1841
Sept 19 Susanna Huffman
         Frances E. Rast
         Sarah Austin
         Caroline Austin

1842
April 17 Eliza S. Fogel
         Mary Zeagler
         Ann Houser
         Caroline F. Haigler
Oct 23   Russel Hungerpielar
         John Hungerpielar
         J. David Rast
         Henry Garick
         DAvid B. Garick
         Joseph Garick
         George Garick
         Albert J. Shurlnight
         Joseph G. Ziegler
         Alex Zeagler
         Christian Gates
         Adam Shirer
         Jacob Keller
         David Stoudenmyer
         Mary Ann Stroman
         Ann Shirer
         Jane Bookhardt
         Mary Pailor
         Ann Watt
         Mary Ann Irick
         Maria Keller
         Ann Carr
         Mary Ann Huffman
         Mary Huffman
Oct 30   Lewis Hair
         Adeline Bradenburgh

1843
Apr 30   David Smoke
         Rebecca Smoke
         Eliza McGrill
Nov 5   Aaron Gates
         Aaron Shirer
         James Wiles
         Lewis Hungerpieler
         Samuel Johnston
         Emanuel Fogel
         Lewis Keller
         Laval Jackson
         John Riser
         Joseph Riser
         Margaret Rast
         Morgan Rast
         Margaret Haigler
         Charles Colsey

1844
Aug 18   Henry Carr

This is to certify that Russel H. Zimmerman has been an acceptable member of the Methodist Episcopal Church at Tabernacle Church of Orangeburg Circuit S.C. Conference.

Feby the 12th 1848

R.J. Boyd, Pastor

CONFIRMATIONS DURING THE PASTORATE OF REV. GEORGE R. HAIGLER

1848

March 19th		Russel H. Zimmerman
March 26th		Clarissa Burke
		Sarah Burke
		Ann C. Haigler
		Mary M. Haigler
		Elizabeth Rickenbaker
		Mary Ann Rast
		George D. Rast
		Mary Hungerpieler, Junr.
		Selena Huffman
October 1st		Jane McClure
October 21		Martha C. Barber
October 22		Emanuel Wiles
22		Joseph A. Keller

1849

May 5th	Lovey Keller
	Jane Keller
	Melchor Huffman
October	Rollin Lane
	Jacob Rickenbaker
	John Keller, Senr.
	Rebecca Wanamaker
	Paul D. Rush
	Henry L. Rickenbaker
	Gideon E. Hydrick
	Caroline Rickenbaker
	William Ulmer
	Catharine Rast
	Anna Rickenbaker
	Jane Rickenbaker
	Martha Rickenbaker
	Samuel Rickenbaker
	Milton Ulmer
	Agnes Haigler
	Hansford Hydrick
	Henry E. Haigler
	Joshua Stroman
	Anna King
	Margaret Waltz

1850

October	James Felkel
	Joseph Barber
	Hannah Barber
	Russel Keller
	Sarah Haigler
	Lawrence Bradham
	Derril Felkel
	Robert Irick, Junr.
	John Felkel
	George Wissenhunt

CONFIRMATIONS DURING THE PASTORATE OF REV. PAUL DERRICK

1859
Sept 21 — William E. Barber
Anna R. Zimmerman
Olivia Gates
Martha C. Wolfe
Oct 9 — Henrietta C. Barber
Oct 10 — Mary Adella Keller (deceased
Oct 12 — Frances U. Wissenhunt
Oct 12 — Ellen E. Haigler

1860
May 2 — Anna Rast (by certificate)
Sept 17 — Elison Gates
Oct 2 — John A. Felkel
Oct 2 — Martha Haigler (to Pinegrove)

1861
May 19 — Mary Ann Eades (expelled)

1862
Feb 12 — George Gates (restored)
Sept 2 — Georgianna Haigler
Oct 5 — Thomas Stillinger (expelled)
Oct 5 — Sarah Stillinger

1863
Oct 6 — Alice Barber

1864
Mar 7 — John C. Harman (certificate)
Sept 1 — Anna Wissenhunt

1866
May 1 — Margaret A. Holman (certificate)
Oct 1 — Emma Holman (certificate)

1867
Dec 1 — Christiana E. Birchmore

1868
Feb 19 — Mary Ellen Gates (certificate)
Aug 30 — Martha E. Keller
Aug 30 — Alice M. Gates

1869
Oct 3 — David Absolum Walling

1870
Sept 11 — Edward P. Haigler
Laurence N. Rush
Henry I. Dantzler
Caroline E. Dantzler
Corrie Holman
Ann Barber
Mary E. Bull
Sept 13 — John Till
Oct 16 — Bachman W. Gates
Ida C. Keller
Fanny C. Felkel
Emma J. Felkel

MARRIAGES BY REV. J.P. FRANKLOW

1799	June 2nd	Daniel Joyner to Miss Margaret Haberman
	June 13	Exekiel Joyner to Miss Ann White
	July 30	Jacob Keller to Miss Christina Houser
	Sep 17	John Stoutenmyer to Jennett Carr
1800	Nov 22	Henry Haigler to Miss Mary Catherine Gates
	Nov 24	Valentine Irick to Anne Mary Gates
1801	Mar 5	John Axton to Magdelen Huber
	Mar 10	John Froelich to Leah Stroman
	Apr 16	Conrad Sauerhaffen to Elizabeth White
	May 3	Jacob Powel to Elisabeth Miller
	May 12	John Garick to Catherine Fogel
	July 2	Charles Smith to Emeline Eberhard
	July 19	Edward Jackson to Rebecca Fitzpatrick
	Dec 29	Thomas Kennerly to Rebecca Whetstone
	Dec 30	John Hoffman to Elisabeth Hair
	Dec 31	Jacob Houser to Elizabeth Hoffman
1802	May 25	Casper Houck to Anne Moorer
	Aug 5	James Hair to Margaret Snider
	Dec 7	Rudolph Murph to Jane Stoutenmyer
1803	Aug 4	Jacob Whetstone to Mary Houser
	Aug 20	Andrew Sellers to Magdelen Whetstone
	Aug 21	Jacob Huber to Anne Kuhn
	Aug 21	John Fogel to Magdelen Houser
1804	Jan 26	Jacob Hoffman to Sophia Zimmerman
	Feb 5	Martin Brandeburg to Catherine King
	Feb 21	Thomas Haslum to Mary Mack
	Feb 26	Robert Wells to Catherine Heckell
	Apr 22	Richard Hardwick to Margaret Ray
	June 5	David Myers to Elisabeth Burkett
	May 29	John Buchart to Miss Hauck
	Sept 27	John Porter to Margaret Genoble
	Oct 18	Andrew Sellers to Dorothy Beniger
1805	Apr 28	Henry Murph to Rosina Stoutenmyer
	Nov 26	Jacob Stoutenmyer to Margaret Irick
1806	Aug 17	John Ziegler to Rosina Speignard
	Aug 24	George Steven Rauch to Anne Garick
	Dec 18	Joseph Holman to Anne Parler
1807	Jan 12	Frederick Gates to Rosina Irick
	May 7	Amos Harris to Anne Stoutenmyer
	July 2	Conrad Holman to Rachell Nodle
		George Ziegler to Rachel Fogel
	Dec 31	David Gilbert to Catherine Piegler
1808	Mar 27	George Charles Rush to Elisabeth de Bardeleben
	July 19	Thomas Sabb to Sarah Frances Francklow
1809	Feb 16	Adam Brandeburg to Sophia Burkett
	July 9	Daniel Stoutenmyer to Magdelen Weis
	Mar 2	John Anthony Menicken to Elisabeth Gates
	Oct 3	George Garick to Margaret Brandeburg
	Dec 31	William Haslum to Margaret Felder
1810	Feb 8	Christian Gates to Magdelen Switzer
	May 24	John Brandeburg to Rosina Ziegler
	June 5	Jacob Ziegler to Margaret Sellers
	July 24	William Garrick to Anne Snider
	Aug 16	John McGrill to Charlotte Gates
	Dec 21	Daniel Fogel to Elisabeth Snider

Marriages by Rev. Franklow, cont'd.

1811	Feb 21	George Osman to Mrs. Ryser
	June 6	John Hepworth Francklow to Mary Smith
	June 6	David Blackman to Charlotte Murdy
	Feb 4	James Daniel Erwin to Sarah Frances Sabb
	May 12	Jacob Garick to Magdelen Brandeburg
	May 21	George Wissenhunt to Catherine Meigler
	July 16	John Roy to Magdelen Hair
	Nov 24	John Wotten to Elisabeth Dash
1813	Jan 26	Andrew Sellers to Mary Brandeburg
	Mar 18	George Osman to Margaret Stoutenmyer
	May 11	Henry Buchard to Magdelen Houck

MARRIAGES DURING THE PASTORATE OF REV. J.P. MARGART

1841	Jan 28	Jesse N. Haigler to F. Caroline Dantzler
	May 4	James W. Barber to Martha C. Shingler
1842	July 24	Aaron Shirer to Mary Zeagler
	Aug 9	Henry Garick to Ellen Huffman
	Dec 8	Dr. R.W. Bates to Elizabeth Evans
	Dec 15	Harmon Weeks to Mary Ann Huffman
1843	Jan 6	Gabriel Felkel to Louisa Hungerpielar
	Aug 31	Joshua Myers to Eugena Gates
	Dec 14	Aaron Gates to Mary Julian Irick
	Dec 21	Henry Carr to Eugena Wannamak
1844	Jan 14	James Wiles to Caroline Garick
	Feb 11	Adam Burket to Caroline Carson
	Feb 22	W.R. Keller to Ann Shuler
	Aug 29	William Bostic to Adeline Williams

MARRIAGES DURING THE PASTORATE OF REV. GEO. R. HAIGLER

1848	March	Lawrence Braddum to Mary Irick

MARRIAGES DURING THE PASTORATE OF REV. PAUL DERRICK

1859	Aug 4	Charles E. Birchmore & Christianna Felkel
	Dec 22	James C. Haigler & Jane Fersner
1860	Feb 16	Esau N. Haigler & Carrie M. Hungerpieler
	May 31	Richard McGrill & Emily Haigler
	July 5	D.S. Haigler & Catherine Stroman
	Sept 6	Henry Rickenbacker & M.A. Riley
1861	June 20	Jacob Bair & Margaret Hungerpieler
1862	Jan 12	Irvin Till & Mary Ann Keitt
	Nov 20	John D. Keitt & Texas Wolfe
1863	Mar 1	George A. Riser & Anna S. Haigler
1864	Sept 28	Dr. M.K. Holman & Emma Moss
1865	Apr 23	William Burket & Ellen Stoutenmyer
	Oct 26	Wiley Wolfe & Ella Zimmerman
	Nov 9	Baid Felkel & Martha Jane Bair
	Nov 23	Elison Gates & Rebecca Pricket
	Dec 14	George Dantzler & Ann Dantzler
	Dec 19	Capers Jones & Ellen E. Haigler
	Dec 20	Charles Gerells & Mary Ann Kemmerlin

Marriages by Rev. Derrick, cont'd.

1866	Jan 11	John Barber & Ann Kemmerlin
	May 17	T. Percy Brandeburg & Eliza Keller
	Sept 6	Josiah Ott & Julia Ann Barber
	Sept 20	Thomas E. Rickenbacker & Cornelia Fersner
	Dec 2	P. Abram DAntzler & Julia E. Fersner
	Dec 20	Michael Arant & Frances M. Wissenhunt
	Dec 23	Judson J. Myres & Emma Happoldt
	Dec 27	F.W. Roberts & Mary A. Eades
1867	May 16	Frederick I. Gates & Mary Ellen Dantzler
	Aug 18	Franklin Rickenbacker & Elizar Wannemaker
1868	Oct 29	Simeon W. Roof & Hetty E. Wingard
	Nov 5	William Haigler & Sarah Shuler
1869	Nov 23	Daniel Weimer & Mary C. Wingard
	Nov 25	John Till & Emmaly V. Keitt
	Nov 30	Labon Irick & Alice M. Gates
	Dec 15	John Brandenburg & M.E. Keller
	Dec 23	Franklin Haigler & Laura Burk

BURIALS BY REV. FRANCKLOW

1799	June 14	Maria Stoutenmyer	
	June 18	Pashly Zimmerman	aged 54 years
	July 22	Maria Mintz	aged 19 years
	Aug 26	Melchior Hoffman	aged 84 years
	Sep 7	John Sneider	about 32
	Sep 10	Mrs. Kumpf	aged 47 years
	Sep 18	Mary Buttler	aged 1 year
	Nov 16	Catherine Zimmerman	aged 53 years
1800	Feb 5	John Sellers	aged 82 years
	May 31	Frederick Mintz	aged 2 years
	June 2	Margaret Mintz	aged 4 years
	July 20	Anne Kennerly	about 30
	Aug 10	John Aron Roy	----------
	Aug 31	Thomas Syfried	aged 2 years
	Sep 2	Mrs. Houser	aged 86 years
	Sep 26	Mr. Joseph Holman	aged 38 years
	Oct 5	Mast. George West	aged 1 year
	Oct 19	Mrs. Axton	aged 24 years
	Nov 9	Mast. John Rast	aged 12 years
	Dec 22	John Keller	aged 18 years
1801	Jan 4	Mrs E. Stabler of Beaver Creek	aged 25 years ----------
	Jan 14	Mr. Jn. Neisler	aged 83 years
	Feb 20	Mr. George Stabler of Beaver Creek	42 years ----------
	Mar 29	Mrs. Peter Miegler	about 30
	Apr 7	Mrs. Bastian Fichter	about 33
	May 22	Mast. Conrad Rast	aged 1 year
	Aug 22	Miss Mary Axton	aged 1 year
	Sep 17	Ann Ziegler	aged 7 years
	Sep 25	Joseph Sellers	aged 2 years
	Oct 2	William Keller	aged 17 years
	Nov 21	John Stroman	aged 57 years
1802	Jan 3	Mrs. Wm. Axton	aged 21 years
	Jan 10	John Huber	aged 55 years
	Jan 30	Mr. Weis	aged 62 years
	Feb 27	Mr. John Hoffman	aged 25 years
	Mar 3	Miss Rosina Sellers	about 3 years
	June 21	Mr. Houser	aged 88 years
	Aug 25	Mast. Samuel Fogel	aged 9 years
	Sep 4	Mast. Ludwig Mack	aged 15 years
	Sep 20	Miss R. Stoutenmyer	aged 52 years
	Nov 4	Mrs. Phillip Harman	aged 50 years
1803	Jan 1	Mr. John Houck	aged 63 years
	Jan 27	Frederick Heckell	aged 57 years
	Jan 31	Mr. John Burkett	aged 43 years
	Feb 7	Mast. Charles Holman	aged 4 years
	Mar 7	William Robert Hoffman	aged 1 year
	May 5	Mast. Stiffelmyer	aged 2 years
	June 8	Catherine Pein	aged 28 years
	June 20	Miss Jane Pein	--------
	July 2	Mrs. Ziegler	aged 29 years
	Aug 20	Mast. William Slater	aged 3 years
	Sep 8	Mast. Stoutenmyer	aged 1 year
	Sep 28	Mrs. King	aged 31 years
	Oct 2	Mast. Ephraim King	----------
	Oct 7	Miss Burkett	----------
	Dec 16	Conrad Hair	aged 32 years

Burials by Rev. Francklow, cont'd.

1804	Jan 16	John Stoutenmyer	aged 30 years
	Jan 17	Conrad Brandeburg	
	Apr 7	Barbara Murph	aged 68 years
	Apr 14	Miss Sellers	
	Apr 21	Paul Shirer	aged 56 years
	May 1	Martin Sellers	aged 39 years
	June 25	Mrs. Wm. Sellers	aged 31 years
	July 21	Miss Anne Maria Sellers	
	July 31	Miss Eugenia Holman	aged 3 years
	Aug 8	Mast. William Zimmerman	
	Aug 9	Miss Juliana Stoutenmyer	
	Sep 22	--------- Zimmerman	
	Oct 17	Miss Margaret Snider	
	Nov 8	Melchior Holman	aged 41 years
	Nov 15	Rachell Wild	aged 23 years
	Dec 8	George Gates	aged 81 years
	Dec 24	Barbara Reichard	aged 26 years
1805	June 9	Rudoff Murph	aged 72 years
	Aug 2	Mary Gibbs	about 42 years
	Aug 5	William Gibbs	aged 16 years
	Sep 8	Mary McCord	
	Oct 17	John Hair	aged 15 years
	Nov 30	Elisabeth Kinlein	aged 75
1806	Apr 5	Catherine Ziegler	aged 31 years
	May 5	Charlotte Hair	
	June 22	Mrs. Rosina Stoutermyer	aged 51 years
	July 9	Sophia Irick	about 11 years
	Aug 20	Elisabeth Huber	about 1 year
	Aug 22	Miss Ulmer	
	Aug 25	Miss Sarah Elisabeth Austin	about 2 years
	Sep 14	Antee Almond	about 4 years
	Oct 13	Martin Gates	about 52 years
	Oct 18	James Brandeburg	aged 3 years
	Oct 24	Mrs. Holman	aged 64 years
	Nov 2	Mast. Reuben Houser	
	Dec 8	George Shingler	aged 84 years
1807	Jan 12	Jane Slater	aged 26 years
	Mar 13	Henry Felder	about 36 years
	Apr 3	Mrs. Fromm	aged 77 years
	Apr 7	Mrs. Emmie	aged 83 years
	Apr 17	Mrs. Rickenbacker	aged 61 years
	Nov 23	Mrs. Hunkelpeeler	aged 95 years
	Nov 25	Melchior Fliegel	aged 85 years
	Nov 27	John Barsh	aged 35 years
	Nov 29	Mary Jacobina Hoffman	aged 71 years
	Dec 2	Jacob Stoutenmyer	aged 28 years
	Dec 6	Jacob Mintz	aged 26 years
	Dec 7	John Hoffman	aged 25 years
	Dec 22	Martin Gates	aged 22 years
1808	Feb 13	Adam Stiffelmyer	
	June 24	Catherine Pein	
	Sep 5	Miss Felder	
	Sep 11	John Myers	
	Sep 22	Joseph Ryser	aged 49 years
	Sep 30	Mary Gates	aged 77 years
	Nov 11	Anne Miegler	
	Nov 15	Mrs. Keller	aged 69 years
	Nov 23	Thomas Syfrid	aged 40 years

Burials by Rev. Franklow, cont'd.

1808	Nov 31	Anne Huber	aged 23 years
	Dec 10	George Barsh	aged 63 years
	Dec 29	Adam Wise	aged 34 years
	Dec 20	John Dash	aged 51 years
	Dec 26	Miss Gates	
1809	Jan 11	Martin Brandeburg	aged 53 years
	Jan 26	Frederick Keller	aged 67 years
	Apr 8	Elisabeth Keller	
	Apr 11	Harman Rush	aged 42 (?) years
	June 10	John Ziegler	aged 37 years
	July 11	John Livingston	aged 41 years
	Aug 24	Joseph David Keller	
	Sep 18	Frances Ziegler	
	Oct 5	Carolina Ziegler	
	Oct 28	Mrs. Christian Gates	
	Nov 7	Mast. Ryser	
1810	Jan 10	Mr. Whiteman	aged 75 years
	Sep 11	William Fogel	aged 20 years
	Sep 30	Miss Zigler	
	Nov 22	Mast. Stacy	
	Dec 17	Martin Irick	aged 50 years
	Dec 18	Maria Catherine Osman	aged 58 years
1811	Jan 18	Eliza Stabler	
	Sep 12	Miss Barbour	
	Oct 20	Mast. Haigler	
	Nov 15	Mast. Gates	
	Nov 29	Abednego Parler	aged 42 years
	Nov 30	Miss Haigler	
	Dec 11	Mrs. Haigler	aged 32 years
	Dec 15	Mrs. Sellers	aged 34 years
1812	Jan 20	Barbara Hoffman	
	Mar 4	Joseph Keller	
	June 12	Conrad Keller	
	July 25	Rachell Houser	aged 44 years
	Sep 29	Margaret Smith	aged 41 years
	Oct 21	Theobald Lentz	aged 71, Rowan, NC
	Nov 13	Mast. Felkle	
	Nov 23	Catherine Barbara Osman	aged 37 years
	Dec 24	Mast. Jacob Ziegler	
1813	Feb 3	Melchior Felkle	aged 51 years
	May 3	Miss E. Anne Huber	Lexington, SC
	June 19	Mast. Jacob Ziegler	
	June 19	Mrs. Gates	aged 49 years
	Aug 26	Mrs. Margaret Osman	aged 32 years
	Sep 6	Miss Elisabeth Pein	aged 13 years
	Sep 6	Mrs. Cubstead	
	Sep 8	Mr. Jacob Hair	aged 82 years
	Sep 22	David Hair	aged 7 years
	Sep 29	John Dansler	aged 74 years
	Sep 26	Eleanora Gates	11 months
	Oct 1	John Pein	aged 8 years
	Oct 4	James Russel Gates	
	Nov 1	Thomas Slater	aged 17 years
	Oct 11	John Russell Holman	aged 6 mos. 2 days
1814	Oct 14	Eve Mary Holman	3 yrs. 6 mos. 8 days
1833	Sep 26	David Luther Holman	departed this life aged 4 yrs. 3 months 10 days.

BURIALS DURING THE PASTORATE OF REV. J.P. MARGART

1841	Aug 4	Adam Garick senr	81 yrs 2 mo 10 days
	Sep 10	Jacob Keller	70 yrs 4 mo 10 days
	Sep 20	Mary Keller, wife of John Keller	
1842	Jan 9	Catharine Wolfe, wife of T.H. Wolfe	20 yrs
	Jan 17	Mrs. Magdeline, widow of Jacob Keller	
	May 6	Mrs. Carr, wife of Henry Carr	
	May 20	Nancy Garick, wife of William Garick	
	Sep 26	Mrs. Catharine Haigler, widow of J.H. Haigler	
	Dec 31	J.J. Dantzler	
	Nov	Mary Burket, wife of Adam Burket	
1843	Feb 23	Miss Burket	
	Mar 30	J.P. Swain, a citizen of New York	
	Apr 7	Widow Burket	
	Apr 25	Jacob Rast	
	May 1	Mr. David Jackson	
	May 8	Mrs. Barbara Stoutenmyer	
	May 17	Federick Kig (or Key)	18 yrs.
	Jun 11	Adam Haigler	72 yrs.
	Oct 30	J. Valentine Irick	70 yrs.
	Nov 18	Mary Irick, widow of Valentine Irick	
	Nov 29	Elizabeth Barber	

BURIALS OF CHILDREN DURING THE PASTORATE OF REV. J.P. MARGART

Date	Childrens Names	Age	Parents Names
1841			
Jul 25	Catherine Holman	7 mo 12 days	dau of T.H. & Catherine Wolfe
Oct 29	Paul Jefferson	5 yrs	son of D.S. & Ann Houser
Oct 30	R.A.	11 yrs	son of George & Margaret Garick
1842			
May 12	Jacob C.	infant	son of John & Isabella Waltz
Jul 20	John Peter		son of Henry Carr
Sep 3	Melchior Abednigo	6 yrs	son of Jacob and Mary Harmon
Sep 16	----- -----		dau of John & Mary Barnes
Oct 3	----- -----		--- of Gabriel & Caroline Carson
Dec 30	---- ------		--- of Dr. Goodwyns
1843			
Mar 22	David Hope	6 years	son of Nicholas & Selena Stroman
June 7	Harriet Eliza	1 mo 2 days	dau of John & Eugenia Mack
Jul 3	William	2 mo 18 days	son of Russel & Eliza Keller
Aug 3	Fredrick Shingler		son of J.W. & Martha C. Barber
Oct 29	----- -----		dau of Lewis & Elizabeth Burkett
Nov 2	Lectra Christena		dau of Adam & C. Rast
Nov	----- -----		son of Henry & Harriet Rast
1844			
May 2	Henry Joseph		son of David & Elizabeth Fersner
Jun 18	Mary Ann Eliza	1 yr	dau of David & Mary Stoudenmyer
Aug 8	Clarance		son of Morgan & Frances Keller

BURIALS DURING THE PASTORATE OF REV. GEO. R. HAIGLER

1848	Names of Adults	Ages
March	J. Martin Irick	
Dec	Amelia Burke	

REV. DERRICKS PASTORATE

1859	Lewis Huffman
1859	Henry Carr
1860, Oct 21	Christian A. Gates
1862, Aug 6	Mary Hungerpieler
1862, Oct 22	Mary A. Keller
1863, Feb 7	J.W. Harmon
1863, Oct 7	Elisabeth S. Haigler
1865, Mar 21	Aaron G. Gates
1866, Dec	Henry Aaron Haigler
1870, Feb 24	James W. Barber
1871, July 19	Frederick Mortimer Gates

BURIALS OF CHILDREN DURING THE PASTORATE OF REV. GEO. R. HAIGLER

Date	Childrens Names	Parents Names
May, 1848	Irick	George & Elizabeth Irick
Sept 1848	Barber	Joseph & Hannah Barber

BURIALS BY T. HAWKINS

Russel H. Zimmerman
Elizabeth Zimmerman
Ann Gates (Caughman)
Morgan Rast
Novice L. Rast
Ann Wolfe

BAPTISMS DURING THE PASTORATE OF REV. GEO A. HOUGH

Date	Childrens Names	Parents Names
Nov 16, 1871	Benjamin Melchior	Dr. M.K. & E. Holman
Dec 17, 1871	Heber Elliott	G.D. & M.J. Rast
Feb 18, 1872	Mary Frances	R.W. & A. Keller
Feb 18, 1872	Charles	R.W. & A. Keller
Aug 6, 1872	James William	P. & E. Brandeburg
Jan 8, 1873	Salena Catherine	M.K. & E. Holman
Sept 6, 1873	Verner Purcy	F.I. & M.E. Gates
Apr 18, 1874	Ann Vernella	J.K. & M.A. Felkel
Apr 27, 1874	Marion Washington Monroe	M.W. Waltz
Mar 14, 1871	Earnest Manly aged 1 mo. 2 days	J.L. & A.M. Rast by Rev. S.T. Hallman

LIST OF MEMBERS OF ST. MATTHEW'S CHURCH REVISED JULY 3, 1872
By G.A. Hough

1. Jacob Harmon   (Dead)
2. Catherine Keller
3. Elizabeth Zimmerman
4. Polly Gates   (Dead)
5. Mary Harmon   (Dead)
6. Catherine Wissinhunt
7. E. Louisa Gates (Dead)
8. M. Julia Ann Gates (dismissed by certificate to unite with Luthes chappel South, Leesville, S.C. Feb 13, 1875)
9. Anna Jane Haigler
10. Frances E. Keller
11. R.H. Zimmerman
12. G.D. Rast
13. Mary M. Houck (transferred)
14. Martha C. Barber
15. W.R. Keller
16. Sarah Bull
17. Dr. M.K. Holman
18. Adrianna Stoudenmire (transferred to Pine Grove)
19. J.L. Rast
20. David Eades   (Dead)
21. F.I. Gates
22. Mary Ann Felkel
23. Rachel Eades
24. Adrianna Sellers
25. W.E. Barber
26. Anna R. Zimmerman
27. J.M. Irick
28. Martha C. Wolfe
29. Henrietta C. Barber (Wyse) (Moved)
30. Anna M. Rast
31. Ellison Gates
32. Georgiana Haigler (to Pine Grove by certificate)
33. Alice E. Barber
34. John C. Harmon
35. Margaret A. Holman
36. Emma Holman
37. C.E. Birchmore
38. Mary Ellen Gates   (Dead)
39. Martha E. Keller (G.B.)
40. Alice M. Gates   (Dead)
41. Ann Keller
42. Elizabeth E. Keller
43. Eliza C. Brandenberg
44. Backman W. Gates
45. Ida C. Keller
46. Fannie C. Felkel
47. Emma J. Felkel   (Dead)
48. Mary E. Barber (dismissed by certificate Sept 21, 1875)
49. Corrie E. Holman
50. Ann Barber
51. Jos. K. Felkel
52. Eugene Barber
53. Adriana Shuler
54. Dr. J.A. Keller   (Dead)
55. James Barber
56. Catherine Wiles
57. Annie M. Rast Jr.
58. Adriana S. Barber
59. T.F. Brandenburg by Hallman (?)

CONFIRMATIONS DURING THE PASTORATE OF REV. GEO. A. HOUGH,
ST. MATTHEW'S

Sept. 9, 1873	James Barber
Sept. 9, 1873	Catherine Wiles
Sept. 14, 1873	Adrianna S. Barber
Sept. 16, 1873	Annie Rast
	Eugene Barber

DEATH OF MEMBERS OF ST. MATTHEW'S CHURCH
PASTORATE NO. 2, G.A. HOUGH

March 9, 1872	Mrs. Barbara Jackson
	Mrs. Alice Irick
	----- Irick
July 17, 1874	Verner Purcy, infant aged 1 year & 6

PRESENT ELDERS & DEACONS
Elected May 2nd, 1875 & duly installed May 9, 1875

Elders

R.H. Zimmerman
Dr. M.K. Holman
G.D. Rast

Deacons

Jas. L. Rast
F.I. Gates
Jos. K. Felkel*

* Bro. Felkel was elected in 1876 to fill vacancy made by death of Dr. Keller.

LIST OF PRESENT MEMBERS OF ST. MATTHEW'S LUTHERAN CHURCH
Made May 4, 1880

Catherine Keller (dead)
Elizabeth Zimmerman
Catherine Wissenhunt (dead)
Fannie E. Keller
R.H. Zimmerman (dead)
Geo. D. Rast
Martha C. Barber
W.R. Keller
Sarah Bull (dead)
Dr. M.K. Holman
Jas. L. Rast
F.I. Gates
Mary Ann Felkel
Rachael Eades (col)
Adrianna Sellers
W.E. Barber (dead)
Anna R. Zimmerman
Martha C. Wolfe
Anna M. Rast
Ellison Gates
Alice E. Barber
John C. Harmon
John A. Felkel
Margaret A. Holman
Emma Holman
C.E. Birchmore
Martha E. Brandenburg
Ann Keller
Elizabeth E. Keller
Eliza C. Brandenburg
Bachmon W. Gates
Ida C. Trezvant
Fannie C. Parlor
Corrie E. Holloway (removed)
Ann Barber
Jos. K. Felkel
Eugine Barber
Adrianna Shuler (removed)
James Barber
Catherine Wiles
Annie M. Rast, Jr.
Adrianna S. Prothro
Perry T. Brandenburg
Fannie E. Holman
Gussie B. Holman
Geo. Edward Rast
Milledge S. Holman (removed)
Claudius J. Rast
Capie D. Bull (Mt Lebanon)
Jane E. Wissenhunt (certificate)
Morgan J. Waltz
Thomas Felkel
John Barber (of Santee)
Willie Prothro
Lena H. Rast
Martha Angeline Waltz
Alice Ann Waltz
Novice L. Rast
Osgood Holman
Jas. Aiken Keller (dead)
Sarah Waltz
William M. Waltz
Dr. Walter Wolfe
David A. Walling
Mary Ella Taylor (Mt. Lebanon)
Anna Wissenhunt (Bozard)
Miss Nelie Felkel
F.G. Haigler
Laura Haigler
Anna C. Holman
Mattie Barber
Elizabeth C. Felkel
Jacob D. Felkel
Russell D. Zimmerman
Geo. Adam Rast (dead)
Jeffie A.D. Gates
John P. Barber
Earnest M. Rast
----- Felkel
Gussie Gates
Heber Rast
----- Barber
----- Barber
Mrs. W.W. Oliver
Miss Georgia Oliver
W.W. Oliver
David B. Garick

Rev. J.F. Probst took charge of Pastorate No. 2, March 1st, 1881

Rev. J.H. Wilson took charge of Pastorate No. 2, St.Matthews and Mt. Lebanon church Jan 1883.

Rev. J.H. Wilson resigned the pastorate charge of St.Matthews and Mt. Lebanon churches Feb. 1888.

Rev. S.T. Hallman took charge of Pastorate No. 2, Nov 22, 1874, St. Matthews Church, S.C.

INFANT BAPTISMS BY REV. S.T. HALLMAN

Date	Names of Children & Parents	When Born
1875		
Mar 21	George Emanual, son of F.I. Gates and wife Mary Ella	Nov 29, 1874
Oct 3	George Edward, son of Dr. M.K. Holman & wife Emma	Aug 28, 1875
1876		
Apr 9	Thomas Houck, son of Dr. J.L. Shuler & wife Amanda	Feb 11, 1876
Apr 30	Harvey Cogswell, son of T.P. Brandenburg & wife E.C.	Oct 6, 1875
Aug 6	Joseph William, son of Joseph K. Felkel & wife Mary Ann	Apr 30, 1876
1877		
Feb 10	Anna Julia, dau of F.I. Gates & wife Mary E.	Aug 26, 1876
May 13	Mary Rebecca, dau of J.L. Shuler & wife Amanda C.	Feb 25, 1877
1878		
Apr 20	Willie Aiken, son of G.D. Rast & wife Mary Jane	Jan 23, 1878
Aug 4	Mary Jane, dau of Dr. M.K. Holman & wife Emma	June ---- ?
1879		
Feb 23	Daisey Rebecca, F.I. Gates & wife Lizzie	Nov 25, 1878
Mar 16	Martha Eva, J.K. & Mary A. Felkel	Oct 27 ---- ?
Nov 2	Maggie ONeall, J.B.O. & Corrie E. Holloway	Oct 2, 1879
1880		
May 20	Mamie Etta, dau of F.I. Gates & wife Lizzie	Jan 17, 1880

REV. J.F. PROBST, PASTOR - INFANT BAPTISMS

Date	Names of Children & Parents	When Born
1881		
Apr 15	Dr. M.K. Holman & Emma L., his wife child - Alfred Wannamaker	Oct 31, 1880
May 15	Parents-J.& F. Parler child - Ozro Harman	Feb 17, 1881
Sep 18	Lizzie St. Clair, child of F.J. & E. Gates - died Feb 22, 1882	Mar 10, 1881
Sep 18	Herbert Luther, child of J.K. & M.C. Felkel	Mar 29, 1881
1882		
Mar 19	Wesley Wiles & wife child - Wesley Walter	Oct 5, 1881
Apr 2	Henry J. Dantzler & wife child - David Anthony	Dec 22, 1881
Aug 20	F.I. Gates & wife child - Thomas Summers	May 22, 1882

CONFIRMATIONS

Date	Namess	Ages Yrs. Mos., days
1876		
Oct 8	Fannie E. Holman Gussie B. Holman George Edward Rast Milledge S. Hallman Claudius J. Rast	10 10 0
Oct 12	Willie Houck (transfered to Lexington) Capie D. Bull (to Lebanon)	
1877		
Jul 15	Morgan J. Walts Thomas Felkel John Barber (of Santee sect.)	
1878		
Aug 20	Willie Prothro Lena Rast	
Aug 27	Martha Angeline Waltz Alice Ann Waltz	
1879		
Aug 27	Novice L. Rast	
Sep 5	Osgood Holman	
Sep 7	Jas. Aiken Keller Sarah Waltz	
1881		
Apr 17	Ann C. Holman	14
	Mattie C. Barber	16
	Elizabeth C. Felkel	15
	Jacob D. Felkel	12
	Interesting communion at St. Mathew's	
1882		
Oct 15	John P. Barber	about 25

RECEIVED BY CERTIFICATE

Sept. 15, 1875 T.P. Brandenburg from Pine Grove Lutheran Church
July 15, 1877   W.M. Waltz from Shady Grove M.E. Church S.
June 1, 1879   Walter Wolfe, M.D. from Wentworth Street,
                Lutheran Church, Charleston, S.C.

INFANT BURIALS

Date	Names of Children & Parents	Age at Death
1876		Yrs., Mos., days
July 5	George Emanuel, son of F.I. Gates & wife Mary Ellen	

ADULT BURIALS

1876			
Feb 3	Dr. J.A. Keller	50 1 0	
Aug 20	Mary Harmon	about 76	
Oct 18	Mary Gates (called Polly)	about 93	
1877			
Feb 2	Mary Ellen Gates		
1879			
Feb 25	Jacob Harmon	about 90 years	
Aug 2	Emma Jane Prothro	18 8 24	
1886			
Apr 30	Catherine Wisenhunt, born Oct 14, 1821, died Apr 30, 1886	65 6 16	
Jul 20	John C. Harmon, born Sept 1, 1826, died July 20, 1894	67 10 20	

DISMISSIONS BY CERTIFICATE

1875
Feb 13 M. Julia Ann Caughman, (formerly Gates) to unite with
        Luther Chappel, Leesville, S.C.
Sep 21 Mary E. Barber, no church designated

REV. J.F. PROBST, PASTOR - DISMISSIONS BY CERTIFICATE

1881
Mar 5   Mrs. Jane Jones - to Bethel M.E. Church

RECEIVED BY CERTIFICATE BY REV. PROBST

Mar 6, 1881   Mrs. Mary J. Rast, from M.E. Church
Jan 15, 1882 Mrs. Ann Caufman, widow of Rev. E. Caufman,
              from Leesville, S.C.

No Record by Rev. J.H. Wilson, 1883-1888

LIST OF MEMBERS OF ST. MATTHEW'S CHURCH
Revised Dec 1, 1894 by Rev. G. Hawkins

1. Geo. D. Rast
2. Miss Lena Rast
3. Heber E. Rast
4. Willie A. Rast
5. James L. Rast
6. Mrs. Anna M. Rast
7. E.G. Rast
8. Mrs. Lula Rast
9. Claude J. Rast
10. Mrs. Gussie M. Rast
11. Ernest M. Rast
12. F.I. Gates
13. Jeff D. Gates
14. Mrs. F.E. Keller
15. Mrs. Margaret A. Holman
16. G.B. Holman
17. Mrs. G.B. Holman
18. T.S. Haigler
19. Mrs. Fannie E. Haigler
20. John P. Barber
21. E.H. Barber
22. James H. Barber
23. Mrs. E.H. Barber
24. Mrs. Catherine Barber
25. Miss Alice E. Barber
26. Miss Ann Barber
27. Miss Mattie S. Barber
28. A.A. Wingard
29. Mrs. Mary E. Wingard
30. Morgan Waltz
31. Wm. Waltz
32. Mrs. Wm. Waltz
33. Jo. K. Felkel
34. Mrs. J.K. Felkel
35. Miss Lizzie Felkel
36. Miss Anna Felkel
37. Jacob Felkel
38. Eva Felkel
39. Jo. Felkel, Jr.
40. Paul Parler
41. Mrs. Fanny Parler
42. Frank Haigler
43. Mrs. Mary Kemmerlin
    (Jas. K.)
44. Miss Carrie Haigler
    (Frank Shumaller)
45. Miss Martha Wolfe
    (Wm. Mack)
46. Dr. M.K. Holman
47. Mrs. Emma Holman
48. Mrs. W.C. Perrin
49. J.M. Holman
50. W.M. Holman
51. Mary Jane Holman
52. Dr. W.W. Wolfe
53. John Brandenburg
54. Mrs. John Brandenburg
55. Miss Connie Brandenburg
56. James R. Brandenburg
57. John K. Brandenburg
58. James W. Brandenburg
59. Harvey C. Brandenburg
60. Minnie A. Brandenburg
61. Mrs. Perry Brandenburg
62. Mrs. (Jos) Hattie Waltz
63. Mrs. Mary Barber (Jno.)
64. Mrs Lewis (Brandenburg?) Jones
65. David Garick
66. John Felkel
67. Mrs. Ellen Felkel
68. Mrs. Fred Buzhardt
69. ----- Buzhard (son of Fred)
70. W.W. Oliver
71. Mrs. Catherine Oliver
72. Miss Ada Oliver (dismissed
    Dec 31, 1897 to Rev. W. A.
    Deatin's charge)
73. Mrs. John McMichael
74. Harmon Rush
75. Mrs. Annie Rush
76. Willie Rush
77. Charley Rush
78. Nina Rush
79. Osgood Holman
80. R.D. Layton
81. Mrs. Salina Layton
82. Mrs. Mary Ann Rush
83. Lawrence Rush
84. Miss Lettie Laytin
85. Miss Zenith Laytin
86. Miss Jessie Laytin
87. Miss Minnie Laytin
88. Mrs. Anna R. Zimmerman
89. Russell D. Zimmerman
90. Capt. J.M. Sellers (dead)
91. Mrs. Adriana Sellers
92. Geo. I. (?) Golding
93. John Holman
94. David Walling
95. Mrs. David Walling
96. W.W. Wiles
97. Mrs. W.W. Wiles
98. Miss Jennie Hawkins
99. Mrs. Henry Jones
100. Mrs. Ida C. Trezevend
101. Martha A. Waltz
102. Alice Ann Waltz
103. Sarah Waltz
104. John Barber (of Santee)

INFANT BAPTISMS

Date	Children	Parents
1895		
Oct 17	Carrie Elizabeth	Mr & Mrs W.W. Wiles
Oct 24	Walter Wolfe	Mr & Mrs J.L. Jones
Jan 12	Thomas Shadrach	Mr & Mrs T.S. Haigler
1896		
Feb 2	Emma Louise	Mr & Mrs W.M. Holman
May 10	Charlotte Elizabeth	Mr & Mrs C.J. Rast
	Mattie Ellen	Mr & Mrs C.J. Rast
June	Herman Hawkins	Mr & Mrs Henry Jones
1897		
Mar 14	John Nichols	Mr & Mrs Wm. Waltz
Mar 14	Lewis Daniel	Mr & Mrs Albertos Bouzard
Oct	Eddie Lon	Mr & Mrs Ed Rast
Oct	Ella May	Mr & Mrs H.E. Rast

INFANT BURIALS

Nov 5, 1896 child of Mr & Mrs W.W. Wiles, buried at St. Matthews Church
Nov 6, 1896 child of Mr & Mrs A.S. Trezevant, buried at St. Marks Church
Nov 17, 1896 child of Mr & Mrs J.L. Barber, buried at St. Matthews Church

ADULT BURIALS

	Capt. J.W. Sellers, buried at St. Matthews Church
Feb 13, 1895	Julia Haigler, buried at St. Matthews Church
Mar 31, 1895	Mrs. Margaret Rast, buried at Haigler Graveyard
May 14, 1896	Henry Rickenbacker, buried at Jericho Church
Feb, 1897	Henry L. Rickenbaker, buried at Family graveyard

MARRIAGES SOLEMNIZED

Gentlemen	Name of Lady	Place	Date
James Heape	Anna Felkel	Brides parents	Jan 20, 1895
J.H. Ocane	T.O. Rast	Brides parents	Sep 18, 1895
T.S. Evans	Minnie Dantzler	Brides mother	Dec 26, 1895
J.P. Dantzler	Rosa Evans	Brides father	Jan 23, 1895
Wolfe Jones	Eva Felkel	St. Mathews Ch.	Dec 1896
Geo. Ulmer	Belle Rickenbacker	Mt Lebanon Ch.	Dec 1896
Elmore Kemmerlin	Jeter Murray	Luth. parsonage	
Ed Holman	Minnie Brandenburg	Maj. A. Holman	Mar 1, 1897

NEW MEMBERS RECEIVED

Name	Church	Date	Mode of Reception
Rose Ella Walling	St. Matthew's	Apr 1895	Confirmation
John David Walling	St. Matthew's	Apr 1895	Confirmation
Herbert Felkel	St. Matthew's	Apr 1895	Confirmation
Mrs. J.L. Barber	St. Matthew's	Apr 1895	Certificate
Heford Holman	St. Matthew's	Aug 1895	Confirmation
Charlie Rush	St. Matthew's	Aug 1895	Confirmation
Walter Wiles	St. Matthew's	Aug 1895	Confirmation
Carrie Haigler	St. Matthew's	Aug 1895	Confirmation
Lula Haigler	St. Matthew's	Aug 1895	Confirmation
Julia Felkel	St. Matthew's	Aug 1895	Confirmation
Mrs. H.E. Rast	St. Matthew's	Jul 1896	Certificate
Mary Parlor	St. Matthew's	Aug 1896	Confirmation
Frank Roberts	St. Matthew's	Aug 1896	Confirmation
Luther Rast	St. Matthew's	Aug 1896	Confirmation
Silas Brandenberg	St. Matthew's	Aug 1896	Confirmation
Clarence Waltz	St. Matthew's	Aug 1896	Confirmation
Charlie Waltz	St. Matthew's	Aug 1896	Confirmation
Lizzie Brandenberg	St. Matthew's	Aug 1896	Confirmation
Maggie Parler	St. Matthew's	Aug 1896	Confirmation
Eleanor Wolfe	St. Matthew's	Aug 1896	Confirmation

The following elders were re-elected June 18th, 1854 for St. Matthew's Church:

I. Martin Irick
Aaron G. Gates
Russel Zimmerman
James W. Barber
H.A. Haigler

A record of the Lutheran members of St. Matthew's Church, Amelia township, S.C. taken in part on the 4th Sunday in November 1813 and in the month of February 1814. I do hereby testify that the subscribers acknowledge that they are members of said church, consequently are under the direction of the clergy of the North Carolina Lutheran convention. February 16th, 1814. David Henkel, minister of the gospel.

Names

1. George Rast) Vestry of
2. Christian Gaits) said
3. Anthony Mennicken) church
4. J. Henry Haigler)
5. Valentine Irick)
6. John Brandyburgh)
7. George Assman
8. John A. Hoffman
9. Jacob Gaits
10. Anthony Fogel
11. John Garick
12. Frederick Gaits
13. Adam Garick
14. Henry Zimmerman
15. Jacob Kellar
16. Adam Haigler
17. Conrad Rast
18. John Burket
19. John Conrad Holman
20. Henry Garick
21. Andrew Sellars
22. John A. Haigler
23. Jacob Hober
24. Adam Hair
25. Jacob Garick
26. John Barber
27. John Fogel
28. Martin Irick
29. George Garick
30. George Wise
31. Mathias Stoudenmire
32. James Hair
33. Samuel Garick
34. Daniel Garick
35. Daniel Stoudenmire
36. Adam Brandyburgh
37. John R. Switzer
38. John D. Gaits
39. William Gaits
40. Rachel Holman
41. Christina Felkle
42. Margaret Switzer
43. Hannah Rast
44. Jane Flood
45. Sussanna Kellar
46. Rachel Meagler
47. Mary Hoberman
48. Margaret Zimmerman
49. Susanna Boschard
50. Rosana Brandyburgh
51. Mary Gaits
52. Margaret Hair
53. Margaret Garick
54. Mary Sellers
55. Sophia Brandyburgh
56. Magdelene Garick
57. Magdalene Gaits
58. Catharine Haigler
59. Barbara Garick
60. Elizabeth Gaits
61. Cebastian Wise
62. Mary Zimmerman
63. Elizabeth Sellars
64. Mary Switzer
65. Mary Garick
66. Mary Pine
67. Conrad Gaits
68. Joseph Flood
69. Andrew Hoffman
70. Lewis Hoffman
71. Adam Wiles
72. Elizabeth Snider
73. Sophia Hair
74. Mary Hoffman
75. Mary B. Hoffman
76. Adam Stoudenmire
77. John Haigler
78. Margaret Zimmerman
79. Elizabeth Minnicken
80. Daniel Kemmerlin
81. Elizabeth Snider, young
82. Jacob Snider
83. Magdalene Buchard
84. Robert Shilling
85. Daniel Sellars
86. John Hober
87. Frederick Pine
88. Daniel Fogel
89. John Buchard
90. William Garick
91. Henry Buchard
92. Joseph Pine
93. Jacob Pine
94. Margaret Rast
95. Margaret Switzer
96. Mary Rast

Members in 1814, cont'd.

- 97. Barbara Pine
- 98. Mary Buchard
- 99. Sophia Garick
- 100. Mary Felkel
- 101. Elizabeth Wannamaker
- 102. Elizabeth Riser
- 103. Hariot Irick
- 104. Mary Irick
- 105. Mary Wise
- 106. Margaret Wise
- 107. Mary West
- 108. William Rast
- 109. George Sellars
- 110. John Slater
- 111. William Snider
- 112. Hannah Rast (joined Methodist)
- 113. John Keller
- 114. Joseph Riser
- 115. Jacob Riser
- 116. Mary Riser
- 117. Margaret Fogel
- 118. Casper Burket
- 119. Elizabeth Meyars
- 120. John C. Stifflemire
- 121. Mary Irick
- 122. Elizabeth Stifflemire
- 123. Mary Siphret
- 124. Elizabeth Rush
- 125. Ann Stabler
- 126. Mary Fogel
- 127. Polly Fogel
- 128. Mary Stoudenmire
- 129. Catharine Hair
- 130. George Balbar
- 131. Charles C. Rush
- 132. Catharine Barsh
- 133. Frederick Rast (to Methodist)
- 134. John Car
- 135. Jacob Kellar
- 136. Catharine Kellar
- 137. Elizabeth Loyd
- 138. Melchior Felkle-to Meth.
- 139. Daniel Stillinger
- 140. Frederick Switzer
- 141. Frederick Kellar
- 142. Catharine Kellar
- 143. Margaret Rauch
- 144. Jacob Seagler
- 145. Margaret Seagler
- 146. Conrad Meagler
- 147. Susanna Burket
- Elizabeth Haigler
- Samuel Gaits
- Adam Rast
- Christian Rast
- Adam Burket
- David Garick
- Rosanna Rast
- Ann Rast
- Rosanna Kellar
- Eliza Kellar
- Lewis Gaits
- Joseph Gaits
- Henry A. Haigler
- Adam Garick, Junr.
- Henry Rast
- James Haigler
- Peter Haigler
- Lewis Haigler
- Henry Switzer
- Elizabeth Rast
- Luvera Rauch
- Elizabeth Switzer
- Mary Gaits
- Rosannah Brandyburgh
- Ann Eliza Hoffman
- Elizabeth Barber
- Margaret Burket

CONFIRMED THIS FIRST DAY OF JULY 1827 AT ST. MATTHEW'S CHURCH

Henry Stoudenmire   Elizabeth (P.?) Bookhard
Joshua Haigler   Catharine Stoutenmire
Wm. C. Holman   Rebaca Brandyburgh
Patrick Haigler   Rachel Ulmer
Christina Felkel   Mary Ann Cates
Seleana Haigler   Rebaca Irick
Ann Wannamaker   Barbary Brandyburgh

NOT CONFIRMED

Charles Stoudenmire
John Wiles
Jacob Cobsted
Martin Stoudenmire
William Sellars
Harrot Car
Elizabeth Snider
Catharine Buckingham
Susanna Burket

THE FOLLOWING INFORMATION IS LISTED AND THEN CROSSED OUT

<u>Elders St. Matthew's</u>   <u>Elders Mt. Lebanon</u>

J.N. Bookhardt
N.P. Haigler
J.M. Irick
Peter Fogle
James W. Barber
Aaron Gates

elected October 1844

The following is a list of the Lutheran Church of St. Matthew's as renewed and corrected from the former one which was in the first Saturday and Sunday in May 1828, now in part Saturday in Aug. 1835.

Names of Members

1. George Rast
2. Hannah Rast
3. Magdelene Kellar
4. Elizabeth Meagler
5. Jn. C. Holman
6. Rachel Holman
7. Wm. C. Holman
8. Henry Haigler
9. Catharine Haigler
10. Louisa S. Stroman
11. Joshua Haigler
12. Josiah Haigler (Removed)
13. Patrick Haigler
14. Elizabeth S. Haigler
15. Jacob Kellar
16. Adam Rast
17. Mary C. Rast
18. Robert Irick (Expelled)
19. Catharine Irick
20. J.J. Kellar
21. Susannah Kellar
22. Valintine Irick
23. Mary Irick
24. Louisa Gates
25. Charles Stoudenmire
26. Henry Stoudenmire
27. Catharine Kavick
28. Barbara Stoudenmire
29. Christina Fearsher
30. Elizabeth Rast
31. Ann Rast
32. Eliza Rast
33. Christian Cates
34. Mary Cates
35. George Cates
36. Henry Bookhardt
37. Elizabeth H. Haigler
38. Eliza Mitchell (withdrawn)
39. Wm. Karick
40. Ann Karrick
41. John Bookhardt
42. Mary Bookhardt
43. Henry Houck
44. Peter Fogle
45. Elizabeth Fogle
46. George Kerrick
47. Adam Kerrick, Senr
48. Adam Kerick
49. Barbara Kerrick
50. Mary Kerrick
51. Sophia Kerrick
52. Euganah Stoudenmire
53. John M. Kerrick
54. Ellin Tolin
55. Elizabeth Rast (died)
56. Elizabeth Ross (died)
57. Mary Hungerpealar
58. Catharine Kellar
59. Rossannah Cates
60. Eliza Rast
61. Mary Harmon
62. Barbara Herrick (died)
63. Elisabeth Snider
64. Henry Rast (Expelled)
65. Adam Haigler
66. Ann Haigler
67. John M. Irick
68. Daniel Hoffman
69. Rosannah Hoffman
70. Mary Hair
71. Mary McClure
72. Mary B. Hoofman
73. Jacob Harmon
74. Jacob Ross
75. J.N. Bookhardt
76. Elizabeth Bookhardt
77. Ann Haigler
78. Margaret Stone
79. Ann (P.?) Watt
80. Jn. Haigler
81. Charles Austin
82. Jane Austin
83. D. Hungerpealer
84. John M. Irick
85. Peter Haigler
86. Lewis Haigler
87. John A. Haigler (Died)
88. Mary Weaks
89. Darkes Wise
90. Rebacak Kellar
91. Henry A. Haigler
92. Casper Burket
93. Adam Burket
94. Lewis Burket
95. Elizabeth Burket
96. Jesse N. Haigler

List of Members, cont'd.

96. Daniel Kerrick
97. Mary Kerrick
98. Lewis Hoffman
99. James Morgan Irick
100. Julian Irick
101. Ann Riser
102. Rebaca Stone
103. Adam Wiles
104. Barbara Burket
105. Hariott Wiles
106. Samuel Rast
107. Wm. Kellar
108. Rachel Kellar
109. Samuel Keebler
110. Nicholas Stroman
111. Mary Haigler
112. Sharlott McGrill
113. Elizabeth A. Haigler
114. Margaret Whetstone
115. Sarah M. Haigler
116. Rebaca Kerrick
117. David Cates
118. John Meagler
119. James Haigler
120. George Haigler   Oct 1836
121. James Barber
122. Elizabeth Kitt
123. Catharine Holman
124. Catharine Cates
125. Mary Cates
126. Catharine Harman
127. Mary Snider
128. Rosanna Jackson
129. Elizabeth Keller
130. Eliza Wissenhunt
131. Mary Jackson
132. Mary Ann Jackson
133. Elizabeth Stoudenmire
134. Mary Irick
135. Louisa Hungerpeler
136. Elizabeth Hungerpeler
137. Daniel Hair
138. David McClure
139. William Watts
140. Eliza Irick
141. Mary Ann Fogle
142. Caroline Carick
143. Charlotte Carick
------ Burket (confirmed 1837)
------ Burket

BAPTISMS OF COLORED PERSONS DURING THE PASTORATE OF REV. J.P. MARGART

Childrens Names	Parents Names	When Born	When Baptized
Mary Elizabeth	H. Wolfs Friday & Mrs. Shulers Bella		Jun 6, 1841
Vicy	Est. Holmans Gabriel & Jesse Holmans Lovely		Jun 20, 1841
Lavina	Mrs. Shulers Charles & Mr. J. Brandeburgs Maria		Jul 18, 1841
Seley Elvina	Inabinets Jim & G. Keitts Syley		Jul 18, 1841
Lavina	C. Gates Jack & Ginny		Aug 1, 1844
----- ----	J.C. Kennerlys Robert & (?		Apr 21, 1842
----- ----	J.C. Kennerlys Manual & J.K. Holmans Rozana		Apr 24, 1842
Francis Ann Eliza	Kenneralys Jim & Mrs. Shulers Amy		May 22, 1842
Wade Sheppard	Kenneralys Jim & Mrs. Shulers Amy	Mar 6, 1843	Aug 6, 1843
Andy Isaac	A. Haiglers Frank & Lewis Haiglers Lucy		Sep 23, 1843
Rias Samuel	Lewis Haiglers Dennis & Adam Haiglers Cate		Sep 23, 1843
Mary Elizabeth	Mrs. Shulers Charles & James Brandenburgs Maria		Mar 3, 1844
James Seipio	Christian Gates Jack & Ginny		Mar 3, 1844
John Francis	Martin Garicks Anna	Jun?, 1843	May 19, 1844
Sarah Ann	Kennerlys Bill & Mrs. Catharine Kellers Louisa	Sep 1, 1843	May 19, 1844
Agness	J.C. Kennerlys Manuel & J.K. Holmans Roxana	Dec 1, 1843	May 19, 1844
Phillis	Adam Holmans Ellick & R. Zimmermans Sary	Mar, 1844	May 19, 1844
Martha	Adam Holmans Ellick & R. Zimmermans Sary	Feb, 1842	Sep 15, 1844

The following information is listed on two separate sheets in the original volume. Both pages have a large cross or X across the page.

BAPTISMS OF COLOURED PERSONS DURING THE PASTORATE OF
REV. GEO. R. HAIGLER

Childrens Names	Parents Names	When Born
Miley	Henny & Senipy	June 3, 1849
Lebedee	Zebbo & Tiller	June 17, 1849
Rins	Teaner & Bob	Aug 3, 1849
Ahrrsitta	Phillis & somebody else	Aug 3, 1849
Lovey	Abram & Lucy	Sep 27, 1849

LIST OF THE COLOURED MEMBERS OF ST. MATTHEW'S CHURCH
Taken Jan 8, 1839

1. Jn. C. Kennerlys Robert
2. Jn. C. Kennerlys Moses (gone off)
3. Jn. C. Kennerlys Sally
4. Jn. C. Kennerlys Katy (dead)
5. Jn. C. Kennerlys Manuel
6. T.K. Holmans Paul (dead)
7. T.K. Holmans Amy
8. T.K. Holmans Nanny
9. T.K. Holmans Roxena
10. Mrs. E. Wolfs Walley (dead)
11. Mrs. E. Wolfs Tinny
12. Mrs. E. Wolfs Fibby
13. Mrs E. Wolfs Nanny
14. Mrs E. Wolfs Betty
15. G. Keitts Margaret (gone off)
16. G. Keitts Harriet (removed)
17. G. Keitts Betty
18. G. Keitts Anna
19. G. Keitts Myers
20. Wm. Kellers Peggy
21. Wm. Kellers Silvy (removed)
22. C. Cates Tuck (dead)
23. C. Cates Lucy (dead)
24. C. Cates Hetty
25. C. Cates Nanny
26. C. Cates Jeffery (restored May 15th, 1841)
27. D. Bernhards Tuly (removed)
28. Mrs. E. Wolfs Amy
29. Mrs. E. Wolfs Hallew (removed)

LIST OF COLOURED MEMBERS OF ST. MATTHEW'S CHURCH MAY 5, 1849

D. Felkels Carson (gone off)
G. Keitts Sarah (gone)
Dr. Keitts Louisa (gone)
33. Mrs. Shulers R. Toxena
34. G. Keitts January (removed)
35. G. Keitts Mary (removed)
36. P. Gates Mariah
37. R.W. Kellars Peter
38. Mrs. Wolfes John
39. Mrs. Wolfes Lavinia
40. C. Gates Lovey
41. J. Holmans Elisabeth
42. J. Holmans Agnes
43. J. Holmans Lovey
44. P. Brandenbergs Nancy
45. Dr. Kellers Sarah Ann
46. James Barbers Amy
47. D. Trezevants Jock (gone)
48. Perry Brandenbergs Jacob
49. Perry Brandenbergs Caroline

A LIST OF THE COLORED MEMBERS OF ST. MATTHEW'S CHURCH
Taken the 22nd of June 1866

1. Meires Joseph
2. Henry Patterson
3. Bill Walker
4. March Holman
5. Walace Fouler
6. Sarah Elick
7. Amy Sabb
8. Harriet Joseph
9. Rochsena Lewis
10. Ann Sabb
11. Lovey Holman
12. Nancy Lowman
13. ----- Wannamaker
14. Nancy Shuler
15. Jenny Adams
16. Wesley Walker
17. Adella
18. Mary Ann Baker
19. Winey Olin
20. Catharine Spigner
21. Eva Ann Caldwell
22. Adison Hoover

Mr. J.H. Haigler received from the Elders of St. Matthew's Church the sum of fifty seven dollars and 81½ cents for P. Haigler. Also received this 18th of July 1833 for Joseph Haigler twenty four dols. 68/100.

J.H. Haigler

Received from the elders of St. Matthew's church the sum of eighteen dollars.

this 18th of July 1833
J.H. Haigler

Received from the elders of St. Matthew's the sum of seven dollars 50 cents.

this 18 of July 1833
Jn. C. Holman

Received from the elders of St. Matthew's church the sum of five dollars this first day of August 1835 by me.
John Bookhardt

Received from the elders of St. Matthew's church the sum of five dollars this first day of August 1835 by me.
J.H. Haigler

Received of the elders of St. Matthew's church the sum of twelve dollars and six cts.

this the 24 of March
J.H. Haigler

Rec'd of the elders of St. Matthew's church the sum of two dollars 25 cts. in full this 24th March 1835.
Adam Rast

Rec'd of the elders of St. Matthew's church three dollars & fifty cents for Sunday School books January 21st 1837.
David Bernhard

Rec'd of the elders of St. Matthew's church six dollars for Sunday School book January 21st 1837.
J.N. Bookhardt

Rec'd of the elders of St. Matthew's church $10.00 for the shingles of the parsonage this 10th June 1837.
J.H. Haigler

Rec'd of the elders of St. Matthew's church this 10th of June $7.00 in full of all demands.
John Bookhardt

An election for elders in St. Matthew's church was held on the 2nd Sabbath in March 1836. On counting out the votes it was found that the following persons were elected to serve 2 years.
D. Bernhard, Pastor

John C. Holman	John Bookhardt
J.H. Haigler	Martin Irick Senr.
Nicholas Bookhardt	Adam Rast

Capt. D. McClure in the place of J.C. Holman dec'd.
Patrick Haigler in lieu of J.H. Haigler.

The following information was on a separate sheet that had a large cross or X across it.

Henry Bookert Dr.
April 18th 1831   To St. Matthew's Church
as their treasurer.................#13 - 2½
(Test) J.H. Haigler

Paid over to the treasurer on the eighth of May 1831 Seventeen dollers & 50 cents.

Paid over to the treasurer on the 1st Sabbeth in Sept. eleven dollers & thirty eight cents.

Collected on the fifth in April Seventeen dollers and fifty six cents.

Paid of last mentioned sum, two dollers to the Rev. John D. Scheck for services rendered on the first Sabbeth in July.

NAMES OF COLOURED MEMBERS
No Date of List Given

1. Holmans Paul
2. Holmans Robbin (died)
3. Holmans Sarah
4. Holmans Sophiah (dead)
5. Kitts Captain
6. Kitts Mary (died)
7. Kitts John (expelled)
8. Kitts Margret
9. Kitts Priscilla
10. Switzers Isaac (removed)
11. Switzers Milly (expelled)
12. Cates Jeffery (restored)
13. Wolfes Walley
14. Wolfes Jinney
15. Bookerts Jack (expelled)
16. Haiglers Peggy (expelled)
17. Dantzlers Bob (died)
18. Dantzlers Charles
19. Wolfes Tobby
20. Kellers Peggy
21. Brandyburg Winny
22. ------- Knight (dead)

Jesse Herrod (expelled)
Kitts Myers
Mrs. Wolfes Nanny
John C. Kennerlys Robert
John C. Kennerlys Moses
Holmans Amey
Holmans Nanny
S. Cates Harriot
S. Cates William (died)
S. Cates Lucy
Switzers, Mary Milley (removed)
John C. Holmans Sonny
C. Cates Tack (Oct. 23, 1836)
Mr. Jn. Kennerlys Sally
Mr. Jn. Kennerlys Katy
Mr. G. Kitts Betty (1837)
Mr. G. Kitts Anna
T. Holmans Roxena (confirmed March 14, 1838)
T. Holmans Anna (confirmed)
C. Cates Lucy (confirmed Nov 25, 1838)
W. Kellers Silvy (confirmed Nov 25, 1838)
W. Kellers Peggy (confirmed Nov 25, 1838)
G. Cates Hetty (confirmed Nov 25, 1838)
J. Kennerlys Manuel (confirmed Nov 25, 1838)
D. Bernhards July (confirmed Nov 25, 1838)

THE FOLLOWING ENTERED ON LAST PAGE

This will certify that Sister M. Gates is an acceptable member of the M.E. Church South on the Orangeburg Circuit.

W.H. Lawton, Pastor
Feb 5, 1854

St. Matthew's Lutheran Church, April 20, 1973. Site of parent church. See plaque below. Six and one-half miles from St. Matthews, South Carolina, on Highway 6 toward Creston, S.C.

"PARENT LUTHERAN CHURCH OF THIS AREA. In 1737-38 the elder Rev. John U. Giessendanner from Orangeburg began Lutheran work in this area; this was continued by his nephew until 1749. By the 1760's St. Matthew's Lutheran Church near here was in use. A later building erected at this site in 1826 was replaced by the present church in 1900."

"THE RED CHURCH"

RED CHURCH RECORD

1767   1838

A copy of the minutes of Vestry meetings of the Episcopal Church near Fort Motte, Orangeburg county, known as "The Red Church", and of other Episcopal chapels in the neighborhood. Copied July 1893, by John Hawkins, from the book lent him by Mr. J.K. Hane of Fort Motte.

Easter Monday, April 20, 1767.

At a meeting of the parishioners at the old church at Mr. Holman's in order to choose parish officers for the ensuing year, when were duly elected:

Church Wardens	Vestrymen
John Caldwell	Thos. Sabb
John Mitchel	Wm. Flood
	Wm. Thompson
	Tacitus Gaillord
	Robt. Willen
	John Lloyd
	Wm. Heatly

1767, April 23

At a meeting of the Vestry held this day at the Glebe in St. Matthew's parish by the Vestry who were all duly qualified by taking the usual oaths - as also the same by the church wardens:

We the subscribers, the church wardens and Vestry of St. Matthew's parish do declare that we do believe that there is not any transubstantiation in the Sacrament of the Lord's Supper or in the elements of Bread and Wine, at the consecration or after thereof by any person whatsoever.

      Signed (as above)

Gave an order on the Public Treasure for 700 pounds due from the Public to the Revd. Mr. Paul Turquand for a years salary, commencing from the 28th day of April 1766 to April 28 1767, and also another for 66/15/10 for parochial money due to the said Parish, both dated April 28, 1767.

Being represented to the Vestry that Jacob Smith, a blind man, is unable to support himself in the needful, they therefore deem him to be a parish pauper and recommend him to be provided for, as such, by the church wardens. Agreed that the Rev. Mr. Turquand do pay to John Loiston, Clerk of the Vestry in the sum of Forty Pounds when he receives it from the Public Treasury.

July 11, 1767

At a meeting of the Vestry and C.W. - Present, Thos. Sabb, William Thomson, John Lloyd, Wm. Heatly, (vestrymen) and John Caldwell, John Mitchel (C.W.)

Agreed that an assessment be made of one shilling and six pence per head on all slaves and each hundred acres of land, moneys at interest _?_ to be paid by the 20th of August next for the relief of the poor of said parish, John Lloyd, John M. Nichol, Samuel Rowe, Collectors.

1767, August 3

Vestry met the Revd. Mr. Turquand and (old vestry) the order on the Public Treasury for 700 pounds was returned by the Revd. Mr. Turquand and another dated this day for 256 pounds, 2 shillings 8 pence given in _it's (?)_ . Archibald Murchy's children to be provided for by the Parish till they can be regularly bound out.

1768, August 30

Agreeable to a public notice given to the Parishmen to meet at the Parish Church near Halfway Swamp in order to choose and elect Parish Officers, viz: church wardens and vestry, and accordingly chose Messrs. Samuel Rowe & John Mitchel, church warden; and Messrs. Tacitus Gaillord, Wm. Thompson, Chas. Rowe, Benj. Farar, Gavin Pou, Wm. Flood, and Thos. Sabb, vestry; and Wednesday the 28th of September was appointed to take in the audit of the Parish Charges, and qualify the said person for the said office according to law. September 28 - Vestry & church wardens met and qualified by taking the oath (same as preceding - signatures as above).

1769, March 27

The church __ and Parishioners met at the Parish Church and made choice of the following persons, viz:

Church Wardens   Vestrymen
Wm. Stent   Wm. Thomson
John Livisten, Jr.   Tacitus Gaillord
                         Wm. Heatly
                         Benj. Farar
                         John M. Nichols
                         Thos. Platt
                         Robt. Willen

An order given on the Public Treasurer for 380 for half a years salary due 25 of March last.

1769, June 1

Vestry met at Parish Church. Present the Revd. Mr. Turquand, Benj. Farar, John M. Nichol, Wm. Heatly, Thos. Platte.
(Those absent at previous meeting were sworn and qualified by taking the oath.)

Wrote to Messrs. John Caldwell and John Mitchell to render and acct. of list and money for the Poor tax the first day of July next, and to will that day choose a vestryman in the room of Mr. Wm. Thomson who refuses to serve.

1769, July 6

At a meeting of the inhabitants agreeable to an advertisement summoning them to meet this day and choose a vestry man in the room of Mr. Wm. Thomson who refuses to serve. Mr. John Thomson was duly elected.
Present at this meeting:

The Revd. Mr. Turquand

Church Wardens	Vestrymen
Tacitus Gaillord	John M. Nichols
Wm. Heatly	Wm. Stent
Thos. Platte	John Livisten
Robt. Willen	

As Mr. Caldwell has provided a Bible and Common Prayer Book for the use of the Church also a blank book for the Vestry's Journal and has now in his hands moneys belonging to the poor of this Parish, it is agreed that the Revd. Mr. Turquand do pay to _?_ the Maintenance of Jacob Smith out of the Parochial money now in his hands, as much as the cost of the above books amount to, and that Mr. Caldwell do stop the like sums out of the Poor Tax now in his hands. Agreed that the Revd. Mr. Turquand provide a Folio Bible and a Common Prayer Book for the use of the Chapel, out of the Parochial money in his hands.

1769, September 14

At a meeting of the Vestry & Church Wardens at the Parish Church - present (names as above).

Wrote a letter to <u>Collr--</u> ? Wm. Thomson desiring him to send the papers concerning the Vestry to Mr. Wm. Stent. Agreed that advertisement be wrote desiring all that have not paid their Poor Tax agreeable to an assessment made July 11, 1767 to pay the same to the Revd. Mr. Turquand by the first day of November next.

1769, October 25

At a meeting of the Vestry & Church Wardens at the Parish Church, present (names above) a petition was signed to be sent to the assembly for money to finish the Parsonage House, the cost of the Bible and common Prayer Book for the use of the chapel.   23 pounds

An order given to the Revd. Mr. Turquand for half a years salary due 29 September last. 380. There received of the parochial money in the hands of the Revd. Mr. Turquand, 57. The amount of the Book purchased by Mr. Caldwell for the use of the church and vestry together with the Register of Births and marriages. 30 pounds.

1769, November 1

At a meeting of the Vestry and Church Wardens at the Parish Church, present (names as above). The Revd. Mr. Turquand returned an account of the Poor Tax he received - 8 shillings, 12 pence.

Which sum together with the money discounted in Mr. Caldwells hand, 30 pounds, was paid to Mr. Jacob Beck in part of Jacob Smiths board amounting in the whole to 38 pounds, 17 shillings. There remains due to Jacob Beck for the board of Jacob Smith from the 13th of May 1767 to the 13th of May 1769 - 71 pounds, 3 shillings. Agreed with Jacob Beck to board and clothe Jacob Smith at the rate of 40 pounds per annum to commence the 13th day of May last. Paid to the Register for 3 years salary out of the Parochial money - 15 pounds. There remains of the Parochial money in the hands of the Revd. Mr. Turquand, 11 pounds, 15 shillings. Agreed that the next meeting be the 6th day of December next.

1770, April 15

At a meeting held at the Parish Church on Easter Monday, present (same names). This day received of Mr. John Caldwell six pounds, six shillings, being the balance collected by him for the use of the Poor and paid into the hands of Mr. Stent who paid to Jacob Beck as part money paid to him for the Board of Jacob Smith. This day Mr. John Mitchel rendered an account of money collected by him for the use of the poor Fifty Eight Pounds, Eighteen Shillings & eight pence. Out of the above sum Mr. Mitchel has paid to the vestry the sum of 20 pounds, ten shillings, six pence which was delivered to Mr. Stent to be paid to Jacob Beck. Balance due still by Mr. Mitchel 38 pounds, 13 shillings and 2 pence.

This day the Parishioners met at the Parish Church - the following persons chosen vestrymen and church wardens:

<u>Vestrymen</u>
Wm. Thomson
Tacitus Gaillord
Benj. Farar
Thos. Platt
Wm. Heatly
John M. Nichols
John Thomson

<u>Church Wardens</u>
Wm. Stent
Thos. Hales

Elizabeth Davis' son made application to the vestry this day for the relief of six small children. Agreed that the church wardens provide for the said children 12 pounds, 10 shillings apiece per year. Agreed by the vestry that an assessment be made on the real and personal property of the inhabitants and owners in P Parish of 3 shillings, 6 pence on every hundred acres of land and likewise on every negro. To be paid the first Tuesday in July. William Stent and Mordecai McMarlin appointed collectors in this district.

John Fisher and
John Robertson

1770, August 6

At a meeting at the Parish Church, present (names as above), ordered that Wm. Stent do pay 44 pounds, 7 being the balance due John Beck to May 13, 1769. This day Mr. Stent paid to Mr. Caldwell by order of the vestry 30 pounds, being money advanced by him for the support of Elias Lever and Joseph Clarey. Ordered by the vestry that Mr. Stent do pay to Jacob Beck 40 pounds, being for the board and clothing of Jacob Smith from the 13th of May 1769 to May 13, 1770. Ordered that 24 pounds be paid to Elizabeth Davis by Mr. Stent out of money in his hands for the use of the poor. Agreed that the vestry do meet the first Tuesday of September next.

October 10

At a meeting of the vestry & church wardens, present (names as above). There remains this day after the payment of the above orders, in the hands of Mr. Stent, of poor tax, 74 pounds, 2 shillings, 1 pence. Gave an order to the Revd. Mr. Turquand for 40 pounds on the public treasurer, parochial money due Easter last. Agreed that the vestry & c.w. to meet on Wednesday, 17th inst.

1771, Tuesday 25th June

The Parishioners met agreeable to an advertisement for the purpose of choosing parish officers for the present year. No meeting on Easter Monday by reason of bad weather.

<u>Vestrymen</u>   <u>Church Wardens</u>
The Revd. Mr. Turquand   Chas. Heatly
Tac. Gaillord   Phil Fryerson
Wm. Thomson
Wm. Flood

Vestrymen and Church Wardens, cont'd.
Geo. King
Jno. Livingsten
Issac Gaillord
Moses Vance

1772, Easter Monday, April 20

At a meeting of the Parishioners at the Parish Church the following persons were duly chosen to serve as Parish officers:

Vestrymen	Church Wardens
Benj. Farar	Wm. Stent
Geo. King	Phil Fryerson
Jno. Livisten	
Wm. Heatly	
Thos. Saab	(sworn on the usual oath)
Jno. Caldwell	
Jacob Christopher Zahu	

Gave an order on the Public Treasurer in favor of the Revd. Mr. Turquand for ½ years salary also for 80 pounds, two years Parochial money due this day. Paid the Register 3 years salary, 15 pounds. There remains in the hands of the Revd. Mr. Turquand of the Parochial money 13 pounds, 15 shillings. Agreed that Mr. Turquand do pay to Mr. Jno. Livisten 10 pounds for officiating as clerk to the church 1 year due Easter 1771. Agreed that Mr. Turquand do out of the Parochial money when received purchase a cup for the use of the sacrament with linnen and if the money will afford it purchase a plate for the same use.

Paid by Mr. Stent to Eliza Davis for her children 1 years allowance due April 1771, Fifty one pounds. Paid further by Mr. Stent to Mr. Hydes 15 pounds. There remains in Mr. Stent's hands after the above payment 47 pounds, 14 shillings, 2 pence. Ordered that Mr. Stent do pay to Jacob Beck 40 pounds for 1 years board of Jacob Smith due May 13, 1771.

Account of moneys due for the support of the poor of the Parish for the year between Easter 1771 and this day:

To Mrs. Davis for the support of her children to this day:	22 pds. 19 sh.
To Jacob Beck for Jacob Smith's board:	40 pds.
To Jacob Esler for attendance & funeral of a man found on the road:	12 pds.
To David Jackson, balance of Elias Lever's acct.:	42 pds.
To Wm. Liviston for boarding Alexander, infant of Simon Kelly:	20 pds.
	138 pds. 19 sh.

Agreed that an assessment be made of one shilling & six pence on every hundred acres of land and the like sum on every slave and in proportion on all other taxables in the said parish for payment thereof. To be paid by the first Monday in August next. James Pierce, Wm. Hill, John Burdell, Collectors.

1772, August 3

The vestry received of John Burdell 18 pounds, 13 shillings, 9 pence being so much poor tax collected by him. Paid Jacob Easler 12 pounds, the same day paid Wm. Livisten 5 pounds.

1773, Easter Monday April 12

At a meeting of the inhabitants at the parish church the following were duly chosen to serve as parish officers for the ensuing year:

<u>Vestry</u>   <u>Church Wardens</u>
Geo. King   Elias Buckingham
Jacob Christopher Zahu   Geo. Hails
Isaac Gaillord
John Caldwell
John Savage
Chas. Heatly
Morgan Sabb

1774, Easter Monday April 4

At a meeting of the inhabitants at the parish church the following persons were duly chosen to serve as parish officers for the ensuing year:

<u>Vestry</u>   <u>Church Wardens</u>
Wm. Thomson   Malcolm Clarke
Chas. Heatly   Geo. Hailes
John Caldwell
Peter Stevenson   (all sworn on the usual oath)

Vestry and Church Wardens, cont'd.
Thomas Sabb, Jr.
Geo. King
Francis Rouche

At a meeting of the vestry on Monday the 2nd day of May at the parish church, present (names as above) the vestry received of John Burdell the sum of 23 pounds, 10 shillings, 6 pence being so much poor tax collected by him. Likewise received of Wm. Stent the sum of 9 pounds, 11 shillings, 6 pence collected by him. Likewise received 15 shillings. Paid Mr. Stent for an advertisement in the Public papers 17 pounds, 6 shillings. Paid Mrs. Davis for support of her children to Easter 1772, 22 pounds, 19 shillings. There now remains in the church wardens hands of the poor tax 19 pounds, 8 shillings. Paid Jacob Beck in hand 10 pounds. Paid Wm. Liviston 9 Pounds, 8 shillings. Agreed that as soon as a list of the defaulters for the poor tax can be made out, that they be put into the hands of a magistrate to be collected according to law.

At a meeting of the vestry at the parish church on Monday, May 23, 1774, present (as above). Then received poor tax to the amount of 42 pounds, 6 shillings, 4 pence per _?_ . Then paid Wm. Livison the amount of his demand, being the sum of 25 pounds, 12 shillings. Paid Wm. Stent for Acct. David Jackson 4 pounds. Paid John Caldwell for acct. Jacob Beck 3 pounds, 5 shillings. Paid _?_ 1 pound, 5 shillings, 3 pence. (Total) 14 pounds, 10 shillings, 3 pence. It is agreed that a list of the defaulters be put into the hands of a magistrate to be recovered according to law without distinction.

1774

At a meeting of the vestry at the parish church August 1, then received by the hands of the Revd. Mr. Turquand from Christopher Rowe 55 pounds, 13 shillings. Received by the hands of Wm. Thomson from Lewis Golson 13 pounds, 7 shillings, 6 pence (total 69 pounds, 0 shillings, 6 pence). Paid Jacob Beck in full for Jacob Smith's board to Easter 1772, 15 pounds, 9 shillings, 9 pence. Received of John Savage recovered by him 22 pounds, 14 shillings, 3 pence. Paid to John Wolrich discount for error 1 pound, 16 shillings, 3 pence. Received further 19 pounds, 6 shillings. Paid Mr. Stent in full for the support of Mrs. Davis' children 25 pounds. Paid Philip Frierson his account 6 pounds, Paid Wm. Liviston for Kelly's child 16 pounds, 5 shillings, 3 pence. Paid Jacob Beck for J. Smith 29 pounds, 5 shillings.

Amount of monies due for the support of the poor of this parish from Easter 1772 to Easter 1774:
To Jacob Beck: 50 pds. 15 sh.
To Wm. Liviston: 24 pds. 14 sh., 9 p.
Contingencies: 20 pds.
(Total) 95 pds. 9 sh. 9 p.

Agreed that an assessment be made of 9 pence on every hundred acres of land and the like sum on every slave and in proportion on all other taxables in the said parish for payment thereof, and to be paid by the first Monday in November next: Henry Felder, Sr., Lewis Golson, Gaspar Brown, Malcolm Clarke and Geo. Hailes are appointed collectors.

That Mr. Thomson do desire the doctor to go and visit the sick boy at Mr. Stent's, its agreed to allow Mr. Wm. Stent at the rate of 60 pounds per annum for the maintenance and clothing of James Corp. It is agreed that Christopher Rowe do provide for the maintenance of Margrett Snyder at the lowest rate he can.

1775, Easter Monday April 17

At a meeting of the inhabitants at the parish church the following persons were duly chosen to serve as parish officers for the ensuing year:

Vestry	Church Wardens
Wm. Thomson, Esq.	John Savage, Esq.
Tacilus Gaillord, Esq.	Mr. Geo. King
Mr. Jac xi? Zahu	
Mr. John Caldwell	
Mr. Chas. Heatly	
Mr. Thos. Sabb, Jr.	
Mr. Isaac Gaillord	(all signed the usual oath)

Agreed to meet on Thursday the 1st of June then to receive the returns of the collection of the poor tax. Agreed that Col. Thomson do take James Corp and that he do send him if possible to the vestry at the next meeting.

June 20, 1775

At a meeting of the vestry, church wardens present Capt. Gaillord, Isaac Gaillord, Jacob C. Zahan, Thomas Sabb, Jr., John Caldwell, Jr., vestrymen; John Savage, Geo. King, c.w.
Agreed that Catherine Jackson shall be upon the parish at the rate of 30 pounds per year and have advanced her on the acct. of the parish 9 pounds. Advanced by Tacil. Gaillord 65, Geo. King 48, Thos. Sabb 67 - Total 9 pounds.

1776

At a meeting of the vestry 6th April 1776 present The Revd. Mr. Turquand, Mr. J.C. Zahu, Mr. Thos. Sabb, Jr., Jno. Savage, Esq., Mr. Geo. King. Agreed that Mr. Turquand do write to the several collectors of the last years poor tax requesting them to make their returns & pay the monies which they have collected into his hands with which sum he is to pay Mr. Beck & Mr. Wm. Liviston their accounts.

Easter Monday, April 8, 1776

At a meeting of the inhabitants of this parish at the parish church the following persons were duly chosen to serve as parish officers for the ensuing year:

Vestry	Church Wardens
John Savage	Peter Stevenson
Geo. King	Samuel Tate
John Caldwell	

Vestry and Church Wardens, cont'd.
Jacob X Zahn
Jos. Palmer, Jr.
Aaron Little
Thos. Sabb, Jr.

1777, March 31, Easter Monday

At a meeting of the inhabitants of this parish at the parish church the following persons were duly chosen to serve as parish officers for the ensuing year.

<u>Vestry</u>	<u>Church Wardens</u>
Geo. King	Jos. Palmer
Sam Dubois	Francis Roche
Chas. Heatly	
Wm. Stent	
Wm. Reid	
Aaron Little	
Wm. Liviston	

1778, April 20, Easter Monday

At a meeting of the inhabitants of this parish at the parish church, the following persons were duly chosen to serve as parish officers the ensuing year.

<u>Vestry</u>	<u>Church Wardens</u>
Geo. King	Francis Roche
Chas. Healty	John Monk
Thos. Sabb	
Jos. Palmer	

Vestry and Church Wardens, cont'd.
Phillip Frierson
Wm. Livingston
Aaron Little

1785, May 16

At a meeting of the inhabitants at Messr. Worley's store by public notice given to the parish the following gentlemen were duly chosen to serve as parish officers for the ensuing year.

Vestry	Church Wardens
Col. Wm. Thomson	Phillip Frierson
Capt. Wm. Heatly, Jr.	Major Derril Hart
Capt. Edw. Richardson	
Major Morgan Sabb	
Capt. Robt. Hails	
Col. Thomas Sabb	
Col. Samuel Tate	

The above gentlemen, except Mr. Hart who was not present, were duly qualified.
"We do swear that I will to the best of my skill perform and execute the office of a vestryman for this parish for the present year without favor, or affection, so help me God. (no signatures)

1786, April, Easter Monday

At a meeting of the Inhabitants of this parish at Capt. Watts by public notice given to the parish the

the following gentlemen were duly chosen to serve as parish officers for the ensuing year.

Vestry   Church Wardens
Thos. Sabb   Wm. Heatly
John Linton   Wm. Watt
Phillip Frierson
Daniel Kelly
Robt. Hails
Morgan Sabb
John Davis

The above gentlemen were all present and duly qualified and proceeded to business.

Agreed that a chappel be built at Bellville, that the old church near the Halfway Swamp be repaired, also the chappell near Campbells be repaired, that subscriptions be made for each respectively and that service be performed in each alternately. Commissioners for repairing the old church; Thos. Sabb & William Watt. Mr. Debardeleben, Col. Chas. Myddleten be commissioners for building the chappel at Belville. Robt. Hails & Phillip Frierson for repairing the chappel near Campbells who are respectively to make out the subscriptions payable to themselves and do their best to have them filled up. Ordered that the church wardens do make subscriptions and get them filled up for the support of the Revd. Paul Turquand for the ensuing year commencing the 1st of June next.

1788

At a meeting of the inhabitants of this parish at the parish church the 11th day of April 1788 the following gentlemen were duly chosen to serve as public officers for the ensuing year.

<u>Vestry</u>
Samuel Tate
Wm. Heatly
Thos. Sabb
Wm. Watt
James Lovell
Francis Lessne
Morgan Sabb

<u>Church Wardens</u>
Wm. R. Thomson
Robt. Hails

The above gentlemen were duly sworn except Thos. Sabb. Ordered that the church wardens do make subscriptions and get them filled up for the support of the Revd. James Farrell for the ensuing year commencing from last Easter. The repairs of the church and chappel to be carried on by the commissioners appointed in the year 1786. Ordered this year that the parsonage house be repaired by subscription.

Samuel Tate & Robt. Hales, Comr.

1792

At a meeting of the inhabitants of the parish at the parish church on Monday the 2nd of April 1792 the following gentlemen were duly chosen to serve as commissioners of the poor for the parish: Messrs. Wm.

Thomson, Adam Snell & Wm. Heatly. At a meeting of the Commissioners of the poor at Abednego Parlor's on Monday the 15th of October 1792, present Wm. Thomson and Wm. Heatly - agreed that the parish be assesed in two pence per hundred acres on all lands and the like sum on all slaves, and all other taxable property in the said parish, and that George Barsh, John Paul Thomson and Col. Samuel Tate be appointed collectors to collect the same by the first Monday in March and to meet at Abednego Parlers and make their return on that day to the subscribers.

       Wm. Thomson - Wm. Heatly

Agreed that Jacob Smith a blind man is unabled to get his living and for that reason he is to be maintained by the parish, and have agreed with Jacob Beck to board and clothe him for seven pounds per year. Agreed that Adam Smith, a poor man, is to be allowed three pounds per year for the relief of himself and family.

     (Signed) Wm. Heatly & Wm. Thomson

At a meeting of the commissioners of the poor agreeable to appointment at Abednego Parler's, (present Wm. Thomson & Wm. Heatly) there received of John Paul Thomson an acct. of the poor tax collected by him - seven pounds, 19 shillings, 3 pence, and of Geo. Barsh four pounds, 15 shillings, 4 pence for tax collected by him.
7 pounds, 19 shillings, 3 pence
<u>4 pounds, 15 shillings, 4 pence</u>
12 pds. 14 sh.   7 p. Total amt. collected
   (Signed) Wm. Heatly & Wm. Thomson, Commrs.

Received this 11th day of May 1793 of Wm. Thomson and Wm. Heatly, commrs. of the poor - 3 pounds that was ordered for me.
                                                    his
Witness: J.P. Thomson   (Signed) Adam (X) Smith
                                                   mark

Received this 11th day of May 1793 of Wm. Thomson and Wm. Heatly commrs. of the poor, seven pounds which was ordered me for the boarding and clothing of Jacob Smith for a year from the 15th of October, 1792.
Witness: J.P. Thomson   his
                         (Signed) Jacob (X) Beck
                                                   mark

Received this 15th of May 1793 of Wm. Thomson & Wm. Heatly two pounds 14/7 being the balance that they have in their hands of the poor tax that was received.
                    (Signed) J.P. Thomson

Belleville - June 10, 1794

At a meeting of the commissioners of the poor at Warley's old store, present, Col. Thos. Sabb & J.P. Thomson, agreed that Jacob Smith, a blind man, is unable to get his living and for that reason he is to be maintained by the parish and have agreed with Jacob Beck to board & clothe him for seven pounds per annum. Also that Adam Smith, a poor man be allowed three pounds per annum for the relief of himself and family.
Also agreed that George Ahger(?), a poor man be allowed for his former services as soldier and for

92

his present maintenance seven pounds per annum; and that an agreement be made with Mr. Jones to board & clothe him for the above seven pounds.
Col. Thos. Sabb & J.P. Thomson being the only two acting Commrs. present, agreed that the money arising from the sale of strays be appropriated to the maintenance of the poor of this parish and that Mr. Wm. Heatly be requested to advance a sufficient sum to pay the arrears due for 1793.

1796

At a meeting of the Commrs. of the poor at Col. Thos. Sabbs - present Thos. Sabb & J.P. Thomson - on the 26th day of June 1796 - appointed the following persons collectors for the poor tax for the parish: G. Barsh, Conrad Holman & Thos. Baldrick, Esq. - also agreed that the parish be assest 2 pence for each slave and the like sum for each hundred acres of land for the years 1794 & 1795.

1st January 1796 - Caldwells old store

Present Thos. Sabb, John Bormia(?), Gideon Dupent - agreed that four pence be paid on all slaves per head and the like sum on every hundred acres of land in the parish for the relief of the poor, and that Thos. Baldrick & Conrad Holman is to collect the same and that the defaulters of 1793 to pay to Thos. Baldrick.
     (Signed) Thomas Sabb
         Dupont
         John Bormia(?)

June, 1796

Received this 6th day of June 1796 of Thos. Baldrick 5 pounds, 7 on account of the poor tax and of Conrad Holman 10 pounds 18 on account of the poor tax. Received this 6th day of June 1796 of the Commisioners of the poor, seven pounds sterling for his maintenance for 1 year.

Witness: Wm. Heatly   (Signed) Jacob (X) Smith
                                     his
                                     mark

Received this 6th day of June 1796 of the Comr. of the poor, seven pounds for the maintenance of Jacob Smith for a year.

(Signed) Jacob Beck

Received of the Commrs. of the poor 2 pounds 4/10½ on account of money borrowed of me.

(Signed) Wm. Heatly

The Commrs. to meet at Caldwells old store the first Saturday in August.

August 5, 1799

At a meeting of the inhabitants of the parish of St. Matthew's at George Killick by publick notice given to the parish the following gentlemen were duly chosen to serve as parish officers for the ensuing year.

<u>Vestry</u>
W.R. Thomson
Melcher Holman
Andrew Heatly
Thos. Sabb
Robt. Hails

<u>Church Wardens</u>
Paul Warley
James Miss Campbell

Vestry and Church Wardens, cont'd.
Adam Snell
Thos. Baldrick

At a meeting of the vestry on the 24th August 1799, it is agreed that a subscription be put in the hands of the church wardens for the purpose of raising a sufficient sum for a support of a minister of this parish.

Agreed that Col. Heatly and Mr. Melchor Holman are to get a workman to look at the church and say what the expenses would be for removing and rebuilding the said church and to make a return to the vestry on the first Thursday in Sept. at the Club house. Resolved that on the first Saturday in November the vestry do agree to meet at Geo. Killicks and that on that day the wardens are requested to bring up their subscriptions.

(signed by vestry as above)

At a meeting of the vestry on Sunday the 29th of September 1799 - present Wm. R. Thomson, Thos. Sabb, Melchor Holman, and Andrew Heatly - agreed that Wm. Austen is to have for the pulling down and rebuilding of the church 35 pounds. It is to be inclosed, the floors laid and the doors and windows hung and a lock to it, and that Wm. Heatly is to draw up a subscription and hand it about to the inhabitants for doing the same, to be paid as soon as the work is done.

(signed as above)

1800

At a meeting of the Vestry at Geo. Killicks on Easter Monday the 14th of April 1800 - agreed that Col. Wm. R. Thomson is to rite to Bishop Smith for a minister - the salary to be 80 pounds - and that Col. Sabb is to board the minister or have him boarded for 25 pounds. Agreed that Wm. Austin is to make a pulpit and pews in the church and the work is to be valued by Messrs. James Miss Campbell and James Butler and if they cannot agree to call in a third person, and that the Vestry to have the pews sold to pay for the making of them and the vestry to meet at the church on the first Monday in August next. Agreed that Capt. Robt. Hails and Mr. Peter Witten is to have the chappel repaired and pews made and the pews sold to defray the expense of the same.
(signed by the vestry & church wardens)

At a meeting of the vestry at the parish church on Monday, August 4, 1800, present W.R. Thomson, Andrew Heatly, Thos. Baldrick, Thos. Sabb, Melchor Holman, Adam Snell, after examining the work of the said church done by William Austin are of the opinion that it is finished agreeable to the bargain & the money now be paid.
(signatures)
Resolved that the vestry do meet again on the first Monday in October next.

1802

At a meeting of the vestry at the parish church 19th

April, 1802, it was resolved that the sale of the pews in the said church take place on the second Monday in May next to defray the expense for building the same, which money is due to Wm. Austin. Sale of pews as follows, all being numbered:

Number 1 - Purchased by J.P. Thomson for 5 pds.
       2 - Purchased by Thos. Sabb Jr. for 5 pds.
       3 - Purchased by W.R. Thomson for 5 pds.
       4 - Purchased by A. Heatly for 4 pds., 13/4
       5 - Purchased by R. Crabb for 3 pds., 10/0
       6 - Purchased by J.W. Goodwyn for 4 pds., 8/8
       7 - Purchased by J.M. Campbell for 3 pds, 19/4
       8 - Purchased by J.M. Caldwell for 4 pds. 13/4
     11 - Purchased by W.R. Thomson for 3 pds., 10/0
                      Total - 39 pounds, 14/8

The remaining pews sold privately by Mr. Austin all but those reserved for the parish.

                     (signed by those present)

1806

At a meeting of the vestry & church wardens of Saint Matthew's parish on the 13th day of May, 1806, at the house of Mr. Conrad Holman the following gentlemen were duly elected:

Vestry	Church Wardens
Andrew Heatly	Jas. M. Campbell
Robt. Hails	Jno. W. Goodwyn
Wm. Caldwell	
Jno. W. Caldwell	
Thos. Sabb	
W.R. Thomson	
Adam Snell	

A letter from the Rev. Mr. Edward Jenkins with the Rules & Regulations adopted by the late State Episcopal Convention were received and considered and unanimously agreed to - and also agreed that the following letter be wrote & signed by the vestry & church wardens and forwarded by J.M. Caldwell:

To the Rev. Edward Jenkins
Chairman of the Standing Committee   14th May 1806

Sir: We have duly received your favor together with the rules and regulations as adopted by the late State Episcopal Convention, in answer to which we hereby inform you that a meeting has been held and subscriptions opened for that purpose, and that a sum of $600 can be raised for a minister, and further accept of your of a minister to preach occasionally for us until one can be obtained. We are, Sir, with respect

      Your most humble servt.
      (signed as above)

1808

At a meeting of the vestry and church wardens of St. Mathew's Parish on the 11th June 1808 the following gentlemen were duly elected:

J.P. Thomson   John Monk
W.J. Myddleton   Wm. Vance

1815

At a meeting of the inhabitants of St. Matthew's Parish on Easter Monday, 27th March 1815, the following gentlemen were duly elected:

Vestry	Vestry Present	Church Wardens
James Lovell	Andrew Heatly	Jno. M. Caldwell
Robt. Caldwell	W.J. Myddleton	Wm. S. Thomson
Edw. Richardson		

At a meeting of the vestry & church wardens at Doctor Mennickens on the 1st day of April, 1815, members present (all as above). Resolved that a church be built say on a piece of land presented by Col. Heatly between the River and Hugers Road.
Ordered that a subscription be raised for the building and repairing of the church in the parish, and that Wm. Vance, Thos. Baldrick & John Tate do contract for the repairing of the old chappell. Wm. J. Myddleton, Edward Richardson & Wm. J. Thomson be appointed a committee for the building of a church as above mentioned. Adjourned to meet on the first Saturday in May at Maj. Avingers.

St. Matthew's Parish
The vestry met agreeable to adjournment at Major Avingers Saturday May 6, 1815 - present, James Lovell, Chairman, Andrew Heatly, Wm. Vance, Wm. Caldwell, Robt. Caldwell, Wm. J. Myddleton. Major Vance from the committee of the lower part of the parish reports that the chapple will require new sills, sleepers, and floor, and new shingling, the

expense of which will be about $150.00. No report from the upper committee.
Resolved that the vestry meet on the first Saturday in June next at Mr. Haglers in the Halfway swamp. Resolved that the wardens be required to bring forward on that day the subscription for the building and repairing of church of said parish and for the support of a minister. Resolved that on that day the building committee report an estimate of what money will be required for the building and repairing of the churches.

St. Matthew's Parish 3rd June, 1815

Agreeable to appointment, part of the vestry met at Mr. Hashun's, say:

Vestry	Church Wardens
Wm. Caldwell	Wm. J. Thomson
Wm. J. Myddleton	Jno. M. Caldwell
Robt. Caldwell	

There not being a majority of the vestry the reports from the different committees could not be received.

St. Matthew's Parish 1st July, 1815

The vestry met this day agreeable to adjournment at Mr. Iricks; members present:

Vestry	Church Wardens
W.J. Myddleton	James Lovell (Chairman)
Edward Richardson	Andrew Heatly

The upper committee reports that they have had a meeting and the contractor, Mr. Vance, has agreed to take down the old church, put it up anew, and whatever material that may be wanted as respects the housing part he is to get himself, the whole of the work to be done in a workman like manner agreeable to the contract made with the committee, say four hundred dollars.

Resolved that the above committee are empowered by the vestry to proceed for the building of said church for the price within stated, the hauling of said stuff to be paid by the committee out of the money, subscribed for the purpose of building and repairing the churches in the parish. No report from the lower committee. The board adjourned to meet at the said place the first Saturday in August.

St. Matthew's Parish 5th August 1815

The Board met agreeable to adjournment - members present - James Lovell, Chairman; Andrew Heatly, Wm. J. Myddleton, Edward Richardson, vestry; Wm. Thomson, c. warden. Resolved that the vestry and members of the within Episcopal society have agreed to have the materials of the old church instead of its being hauled as above stated, to the spot where said church is to be built.

St. Matthew's Parish 10th November 1816

The vestry met agreeable to order - members present - James Lovell, Chairman; Andrew Heatly, Wm. Caldwell, Robt. Caldwell, W.J. Myddleton, vestry; W.J. Thomson, warden. Resolved that John T. McCord be appointed clerk of the vestry of the said parish. The vestry appointed the 24th of December next for the vestry, wardens, and members to meet at Mr. Iricks, and ajourned.

St. Matthew's Parish 24th December, 1816

The vestry met agreeable to appointment. Present - James Lovell, chairman, Ed. Richardson, W.J. Myddleton, & Robt. Caldwell, vestry; and W.J. Thomson, J.M. Caldwell, wardens. Resolved that the pews of the Episcopal church of St. Matthew's Parish be sold on the 11th of January next if not otherwise disposed of.

1818, January 22

Agreeable to previous appointment, the vestry met at Mr. Iricks. The members met are the following:

Vestry	Church Wardens
Col. Heatly	W.L. Thomson
James Lovell, chairman	
W.J. Myddleton	
Ed Richardson	

Resolved that Col. Edward Richardson be appointed delegate for the year 1818 to meet the convention at Charleston.
Resolved that the wardens of the Protestant Episcopal church of St. Matthew's parish do forward a subscription for defraying expenses of the convention.
Resolved that the vestry meet at the church every Sunday and one previously appointed read the service

and a sermon to the congregation. This to commence 1st February 1818. The vestry appointed the first Saturday in March for their next meeting at Mr. Iricks - there adjourned.

1819 - 25 May

The vestry and church wardens met at the parish church, members present - James Lovell, chairman, Andrew Heatly, Ed. Richardson, W.J. Myddleton & W.J. Thomson, wardens. The Revd. Francis De La Vaux was unanimously elected rector of St. Mathews Parish. Resolved that the Revd. Mr. DeLaVaux receive for his salary for the year 1819 one thousand dollars, and that the year commence from the 7th of April last. Resolved that the pews be assessed for the present year at ten dollars per pew for the large, and five dollars per pew for the small pews. Resolved that the building committee immediately proceed to have the church lathed and plastered and the windows glazed. On motion ordered that another vestryman be elected to fill the vacancy occassioned by the removal of Major Vance when Mr. __?__ Stuart was unannimously elected. Mr. J. Lovell then resigned his seat as a vestryman of T Parish. Paid into the hands of Col. E. Richardson by Mr. W.T. Thomson $10.00, Mr. E. Thomson $10.00, and Col. A. Heatly $15.00 as their pew rent for the year 1819 - November 21, 1819, the above sum received by Col. Richardson has been paid (by said Richardson) to Gordan for plastering the church - also $10.00 by Mr. Lovell and $5.00 by Col. Richardson - all to Gordon.

St. Matthew's Parish
Diocese of So. Carolina

Whereas it had become inconvenient to the inhabitants of this parish, severally to attend Divine Service in the Parish Church where it originally was placed, and where as it therefore seemed expedient to them to remove it to the site of this building, being land given by Col. Andrew Heatly for the purpose, and whereas it has been declared to me to be the wish of the vestry of this parish that the church, agreeably to the desire of the inhabitants, has been removed to this site and thereon duly refilled and repaired, should be consecrated by the name St. Matthew's Church - Now therefor, <u>be it known to all whom it may concern,</u> that this church is from and forever after the date hereof, set apart from all common, temporal, and worldly uses, to be a place for the worship of <u>God Almighty, the Father, Son, and Holy Ghost,</u> according to the rites of the Protestant Episcopal Church in the United States of America, being dedicated to God for such only use, in the manner prescribed by the Liturgy of the said Church, by the name and title St. Matthew's Church, St. Matthew's Parish.
Done this day, the twenty-first of November in the year of our Lord one thousand eight hundred and nineteen, and in the second of my consecration.
(Signed) Nathaniel Bowen
Bishop of the Protestant Episcopal Church in S.C.

1820, February 20

The vestry met agreeable to appointment at the church. Members present: Wm. J. Myddleton, Chairman,

Andrew Heatly, Ed. Richardson, W. T. Thomson, (warden). Resolved that Maj. E. Haskele be appointed delegate for the year 1820 to meet the convention at Charleston. Resolved that Col. E. Richardson be authorized to contract for the repairing of Mr. DeLaVaux house, and each member of the church be bound to pay an equal proportion of the expense of the same.

1820, April 15

At a meeting of the Parishioners of St. Matthew's Parish this day they went into the following resolutions, viz:
As the necessary business of the church very frequently suffers serious delay from the difficulty of forming a quorum of the vestry, their number being too large and extended too far over the parish to be convenient to attend regularly and particularly so on trivial occassions, therefore resolved, that in future the number which is at present seven, shall consist of five vestrymen and two wardens. They then went into an election for vestry and wardens to serve until the Easter Monday 1821. On counting the votes the following persons were unanimously elected:

Vestry
Col. A. Heatly
Mr. Wm. Caldwell
Mr. James Stuart
Col. W.J. Myddleton
Col. E. Richardson

Church Wardens
Mr. W.T. Thomson
Mr. J.M. Caldwell

1821, April 23

Being Easter Monday, the day on which the vestry and wardens are usually elected, the Parishioners present went into the election. On counting the votes over the following persons were found unanimously elected:

Vestry	Church Wardens
Robt. Caldwell	Jno. M. Caldwell
James Stuart	W.T. Thomson
Charles Thomson	
Jno. T. McCord	
Edw. Richardson	

Then Adjourned till 15th day of May.

1822, 8th April

Being Easter Monday the Parishioners met and went into an election for vestry men and wardens and the following persons were elected:

Vestry	Church Wardens
Robt. Caldwell	Jno. M. Caldwell
James Stuart	W.T. Thomson
Chas. Thomson	
Jno. T. McCord	
Edw. Richardson	

1823, January 27

At a meeting of the Parishioners and vestry this day held at the parish church they raised a subscription for the support of the Rector, the pay of the sexton

and the rent of the Glebe, in the following manner, and subscribed as hereafter recorded - viz:
We the subscribers do promise to pay the sums annexed to our names for the support of the Rector, the pay of the sexton and rent of the Glebe, the payments being due half yearly, to be paid to the Rector viz: on the 15th day of November the first payment, and the 8th of April the balance. Done at the Parish church the day and year above mentioned and signed by:

Andrew Heatly	$150	James Lovell	$102½
James Stuart	67½	Wm. L. Lewis	42½
J.M. Caldwell	32½	Jno. T. McCord	42½
Robt. Caldwell	32½	Elizabeth Thomson	42½
Chas. R. Thomson	22½	Robt. H. Goodwyn	22½
Wm. T. Thomson	52½	Ed. Richardson	102½
Martha Goodwyn	42½	Jno. L. Thomson	27½

I certify this to be a correct copy.
     Ed. Richardson
The vestry then went into an election for a delegate to serve in the convention for the Diocese of So. Carolina, when Edward Richardson was elected for the year 1823. The vestry then adjourned. _?_ .

1824, Easter Monday

The parishioners met this day and elected:

Vestry	Church Wardens
James Stuart	Wm. T. Thomson
Chas. R. Thomson	Jos. R. McCord
John T. McCord	
Robt. Caldwell	
Ed. Richardson	

1825, January 20

The vestry met according to appointment and Major E. Haskele was duly elected delegate to the convention.

1825, Easter Monday

The parishioners met this day and elected:

Vestry	Church Wardens
James Lovell	Wm. J. Thomson
Andrew Heatly	Jos. R. McCord
C.R. Thomson	
Wm. L. Lewis	
Ed. Richardson	

1826, January 26

The vestry met agreeable to appointment and elected Ed. Richardson to serve in the convention for this year.

1827, Easter Monday

The parishioners met this day and elected:

Vestry	Church Wardens
Wm. L. Lewis	Wm. T. Thomson
C.R. Thomson	Jos. R. McCord
Thos. Hrabowski	
R.H. Goodwyn	
Ed. Richardson	

1828, Easter Monday

The parishioners met and elected:

Vestry	Church Wardens
Wm. L. Lewis	Wm. T. Thomson
C.R. Thomson	J.R. McCord
R.H. Goodwyn	
T.T. Hrabowski	
Ed. Richardson	

1829, 17th January

The vestry met by appointment given and James T. Miles was duly elected to serve in the convention for this year.

1829, Easter Monday

The parishioners met according to custom and elected:

Vestry	Church Wardens
W.L. Lewis	Wm. S. Thomson
C.R. Thomson	Jos. R. McCord
R.H. Goodwyn	
Jas. T. Miles	
Ed. Richardson	

1835, Easter Monday

The parishioners met according to appointment and elected:

Vestry	Church Wardens
James T. Miles	C.R. Thomson
Wm. S. Thomson	Ed. Richardson
Wm. L. Lewis	

Vestry and Church Wardens, cont'd.
R.H. Goodwyn
Jos. R. McCord
The vestry then elected James T. Miles chairman of the vestry and adjourned.

TOTNESS

1830, January 13

The vestry met at Totness and agreed to hand around a subscription for the building of a place of worship in the village of Totness.
The following persons subscribed the sum annexed to their names:

Mrs. Ann Lovell	$60	- paid
Mrs. Elizabeth Thomson	25	- paid
Col. Ed. Richardson	50	- paid
Capt. Wm. L. Lewis	35	- paid
Wm. T. Thomson	25	- paid
Chas. R. Thomson	20	- paid
Dr. Robt. H. Goodwyn	10	- paid
Jas. T. Miles	5	- paid
Dr. Thos. J. Goodwyn	5	- paid
Dr. V.D. Junerson	10	- paid
Thos. T. Hrabowski	10	- paid
Miss Ann Hrabowski	15	- paid
Geo. Butler	10	- paid
Mr. H. Reid	10	- paid
R.P. McCord	5	- paid
Jos. R. McCord	5	- paid

The vestry then agreed with Col. Ed Richardson to build a house for the purpose above mentioned and to give him the amount subscribed for the same.

The vestry then adjourned.

Totness - July 7, 1830

The Vestry by appointment met at the house just erected for a place of public worship and agreed to receive the building from Col. Ed. Richardson, it being finished according to contract. The vestry then proceeded to number the benches and draw for seats. The following is the order in which the numbers were drawn:

Name	No.	Name	No.
Capt. Wm. L. Lewis	1	Dr. Thos. J. Goodwyn	9
Mrs. H. Reid	2	Col. Ed Richardson	10
R.P. McCord	3	Mrs. E. Thomson	11
Thos. T. Hrabowski	4	Dr. V. Junerson	12
Geo. Butler	5	Dr. Robt. H. Goodwyn	13
Mrs. Ann Lovell	6	Wm. T. Thomson	14
Miss Ann Hrabowski	7	Jas. T. Miles	15
Chas. R. Thomson	8	Jos. R. McCord	16

The vestry then adjourned - an arrangement having been made with some of the seats. The same were set apart for the present as publick to which all the inhabitants around Totness have been publickly invited.

Totness, July 11

The Vestry met according to appointment at Col. Ed. Richardsons and walked in procession to the building lately erected for devine worship (The Revd. Mr. Wm. L. Wilson being the rector of our parish church) dedicated the same to the worship of Almighty God, until the same should be regularly consecrated by the

Bishop of the Diocese. The vestry then adjourned.

Totness, October 24

The vestry met (according to appointment made the evening before) at the village chapel where they received the Right Revd. Nathaniel Bowen (Bishop of the P.E. Church in So. Carolina) who being regularly inducted into the chapel, he administered the rite of Consecration as the following sentence will show:

1830   TOTNESS
                       Diocese of S. Carolina

Whereas the members of the Protestant Episcopal Church inhabiting St. Matthew's Parish, have for many successive years resorted to pine land in the upper part of the parish to which the name of Totness has been given, as a place of healthy residence during the summer and whereas such inhabitants of Totness had found themselves subjected to much inconvenience for want of a suitable place of worship, and at length by a subscription had among themselves (assisted by a few of the other denominations) have provided themselves a building for the purposes of their religious assembeling, and the vestry of the parish in behalf of the said inhabitants and subscribers, have requested and authorized the consecration of the said building according to the form and manner of the Protestant Episcopal Church in the United States:
Now, therefore, be it known to all men, that from the date of this instrument the building as above provided

being sufficiently finished for use as a place of worship is set apart from all common and un hallowed uses, to be a house sacred to the Lord, to be occupied by the members of the Protestant Episcopal Church in St. Matthew's Parish in worshipping him according to the Liturgy of that Church and receiving religious instruction according to its doctrine (no others being without its express and duly authorized permission to be admitted & that no otherwise than occasionally to the use of it) and to be designated and known by the name and title of Totness Chapel, St. Matthew's Parish.

Given this 24th day of October, in the year of our Lord, one thousand eight hundred and thirty at the above named chapel. James T. Miles being chairman of the vestry of the parish, Wm. T. Thomson, Wm. L. Lewis, Robt. H. Goodwyn & Jos. R. McCord, Esqs. being the other vestrymen and Chas. R. Thomson & Edw. Richardson, Esqs. being church wardens.

 (Signed) Nathaniel Bowen
 Bishop of the P.E. Church in So. Carolina

1831, April 4

Being Easter Monday, the parishioners met at the parish church and elected the following gentlemen vestry and wardens:

Vestry	Church Wardens
Wm. T. Thomson	Col. Ed. Richardson
Wm. L. Lewis	Chas. R. Thomson
Dr. R.H. Goodwyn	
Jos. R. McCord	
Jas. T. Miles	

The vestry then elected Jas. T. Miles chairman. The chairman was requested to answer the letter from the secretary of the P.E. Convention ? what is the amt. now due from the Church of St. Matthew's to the P.E. church in the Diocese of So. Carolina. Adjourned ? .

1831, May 22

The vestry met this day by appointment at the P. Church, present Wm. T. Thomson, Wm. L. Lewis, Robt. H. Goodwyn, Ed. Richardson, Jas. T. Miles, when the necessity and expediency of erecting a building at Totness for the residence of the Rector of the Parish was taken up, and on motion of J.T. Miles, chairman unanimously resolved that Col. Ed. Richardson and Mr. W.T. Thomson be authorized and requested to contract for the building of said house and report to the vestry the requisite sum for said work and that the same shall be paid by subscription. Vestry adjourned ____?____ .

Totness, August 6, 1831

The vestry met this day by appointment at the chapel and having received the report of the committee appointed to have a house erected at Totness for the residence of the Rector - agree to receive the said building at the sum of Three Hundred and Twenty Five Dollars ($325). On motion of Wm. L. Lewis it was resolved that whereas Mr. Wm. T. Thomson and Col. Ed. Richardson have erected the said building for the sum of $325, resolved that the subscriptions when recd. to said amt. to be paid over by the collecting warden to the said Thomson & Richardson. The chairman was then requested to record a copy of the subscription and the vestry adjourned.

Copy of the subscription to the building of a house at Totness for the residence of the Rector of the Parish.

We the subscribers, promise to pay the sums annexed to our names to Col. Wm. T. Thomson and Col. Ed. Richardson for building a house for the Rector (of the Parish) at Totness. Given under our hands this 6th day of August 1831:

Mrs. E. Thomson	$50	- paid
Wm. L. Lewis	50	- paid
Chas. R. Thomson	25	- paid
Ann Lovell	60	- paid
R.H. Goodwyn	25	- paid
Ed. Richardson)		
Wm. T. Thomson)	50	- paid
Chas. T. Haskell	15	- paid
Wm. A. Goodwyn	20	- paid
Jas. T. Miles	5	- paid
Thos. T. Hrabowski	10	- paid
T. (or I.) Warley	5	- paid
Total -	$315	

1832, April 23

Being Easter Monday the parishioners met at the Parish church and elected the following officers:

Vestry	Church Wardens
Wm. T. Thomson	Col. Ed. Richardson
Wm. L. Lewis	Chas. R. Thomson
Dr. Robt. H. Goodwyn	

Vestry and Church Wardens, cont'd.
Jos. R. McCord
Jas. T. Miles
Jas. T. Miles elected chairman of the vestry.

1833, January 20

The vestry met according to appointment, Col. Ed. Richardson being requested to serve in convention for this year and was duly elected delegate.

April 8

Being Easter Monday the parishioners met at the Parish Church and elected the following gentlemen vestry and wardens:

Vestry   Church Wardens
Wm. T. Thomson   Col. Ed Richardson
Wm. L. Lewis   Chas. R. Thomson
Dr. R.H. Goodwyn
Jos. R. McCord
Jas. T. Miles

None of the vestry being present no chairman was elected.

Totness, July 6, 1833

The vestry met this day at the chapel by a special call of the chairman, present (all but McCord and Goodwyn) Mrs. Ann Lovell made the following communication to the vestry through Col. Ed. Richardson. That she had procured a bell and its appendages from New York which she now presented to the vestry for the use of the church or chapel at this place. On motion of Jas. T. Miles, resolved, that the vestry do accept the bell presented by Mrs. Lovell, that arrangements be made to erect a cupola for the convenience of hanging the said bell; and that a committee of two be appointed to wait on Mrs. Lovell to express the thanks of the vestry to that Lady for the estimable present - whereupon Mr. Wm. T. Thomson and Capt. Wm. L. Lewis were appointed that committee. The said committee reported that they had performed the duty assigned them. The vestry then adjourned. The cupala was erected by the liberality of Capt. Wm. L. Lewis who generously agreed to finish the same without cost or expense to the vestry and Mr. Geo. Butler liberally gave the materials for the same.

1834, March 31 - Saint Matthew's

Being Easter Monday the parishioners met at the parish church and elected the following officers:

Vestry	Church Wardens
Col. Ed. Richardson	Robt. H. Goodwyn
Wm. T. Thomson	Wm. L. Lewis
Chas. R. Thomson	
Thos. J. Goodwyn	
James T. Miles	

The vestry then elected Mr. Miles chairman and secretary.

May 11th
Our minister, Mr. William T. Wilson, died on this day.

August

The vestry met at the chapel at Totness and agreed that the Revd Mr. Peter J. Shand(?) of Columbia, So. Ca. should be invited to officiate for us in our chapel at Totness during the remainder of the season whenever convenient for him to leave his congregation. Mr. Shand(?) did visit us twice during the remainder of the season performing service three times on each day, much to the satisfaction of the entire congregation.

Sep. 25

The vestry met at Col. Richardsons after service at the chapel by Mr. Shand(?) and it being stated that Mr. S(?) had lost his horse on his visit to our congregation, a subscription was immediately handed around to the congregation in order to reinstate his loss, and $111. being received. It was tendered to him by the vestry through its chairman but refused by Mr. Shand(?) in a very feeling manner. Said amount has since been vested for the good of Mr. Shand(?) During the summer of this year, 1834, our chapel at Totness was very neatly painted white on the outer part by the liberality of Col. Wm. L. Lewis furnishing paint and painter gratis.

At a meeting of the vestry during this summer it was agreed that the former Rector Mr. Wm. T. Wilson died entitled to one quarters salary and that the same be collected and paid to his widow. The following is a statement of what was due by each subscriber according to the annual subscription:

Mrs. Ann Lovell $37.50   Col. Ed Richardson $37.50
Col. Wm. L. Lewis 20.00   Col. Wm. T. Thomson 15.00

Subscriptions for Mr. Wilson, cont'd.
Mrs. Elizabeth Thomson $12.50   Wm. E. Haskell   12.50
Col. R.H. Goodwyn   7.50   Chas. R. Thomson   6.25
Jas. T. Miles   3.75   Thos. Worley   2.50
Total - $154.95

September 10
A communication was this day recd. from the Bishop relative to the wish of the Rev. Mr. McKinney (a minister from Maryland) to visit our parish and to know on what terms he would be received among us. An answer was returned by the vestry through their chairman a copy of which letter together with the Bishop's communication is with this board.

December 11
The Rev. Mr. McKinney came up from Charleston on a visit to the parish, remained until the 23rd. An offer was made by the vestry for his taking charge of the church which has since been declined.

1835, February 11
The vestry met at the parish church and agreed to invite the Revd. Mr. Richard Johnson of Beaufort, So. Ca. to the charge of our church and allow him $600 from first of March to January 1st next. Said amount to be raised by subscription. The said offer has been accepted by Mr. Johnson.

1835, April 20
Being Easter Monday the parishioners met and elected the following officers:

<u>Vestry</u>   <u>Church Wardens</u>
E. Richardson   R.H. Goodwyn
W.T. Thomson   W.L. Lewis
C.R. Thomson
T.J. Goodwyn
W.E. Haskell

Mr. J.T. Miles having declined reelection both as vestryman and chairman, much to the regret of the meeting, all the above members being present a subscription was entered into for the support of our Rector for the ensuing year to commence on the first of May 1835 and ending on 1st. January 1836. The following sums were subscribed for the under mentioned persons.

W.T. Thomson	$100 - paid	
T. J. Goodwyn	20 - paid	
W.L. Lewis	85 - paid	
Mrs. C. Haskell	20 - paid	
C. Thomson	50 - paid	
E. Richardson	150 - paid	(per Miles)
L. Cheeves	50 - paid	(per W. Haskell)
C.R. Thomson	40 - paid	
N.T. Darby	20 - paid	
W.E. Haskell	50 - paid	
R.H. Goodwyn	25 - paid	
J.T. Miles	10 - paid	
Mrs. Warley	10 - paid	
J. Dallas	50 - paid	(per Haskell)

And no further business being before the meeting they adjourned.

1836, August 10

The vestry met this day pursuant to adjournment and the following subscription was made for the support of the minister of the year, 1836.

Dr. A.T. Darby	$23.25
Dr. T.J. Goodwyn	23.25
Jas. Noble	23.25
Mrs. C. Haskell	23.25
Mrs. J. Rutledge	23.25
W.E. Haskell	57.75
R.H. Goodwyn	34.75
Jas. T. Miles	11.75
E. Richardson	172.75
C.R. Thomson	69.25
W.T. Thomson	115.25
Mrs. E. Thomson	57.75
W.L. Lewis	115.25
Total	$750.75

INDEX

ADAMS, Jenny(C),064
AHGER(?), George,092
ALMOND, Antee,043
ARANT, Frances M.,019 ,041
, Michael,041
ASSMAN, George,057
AUSTEN, Wm.,095
AUSTIN, Caroline,017,036
, Charles,015,060
, Chas.Shadrack,007
, Jane,015,017,060
, Mary Elisabeth,005
, Mary,005,009
, Sarah Elisa.,043
, Sarah,017 ,036
, William,005,009,096
, Wm.,096,097
AVINGERS, (Maj),099
AXTON, (Mrs),042
, Elisabeth I.,004
, John,004,039
, Magdelen,039
, Mary,005,042
, Wm.(Mrs),042
BAIR, Jacob,040
, Margaret,040
, Martha Jane,040
BAKER, Mary Ann(C),064
BALBAR, George,058
BALDRICK, Thos.,093,094,095,096,
099
BALLARD, John,008
BARBER, ,050
, Adriana S.,023 ,048
, Adriana T.,024
, Adrianna S.,021,049
, Alice E.,048,050,054
, Alice Eliz.,023
, Alice,019 ,038
, Ann,038,041,048,050,054
, Aron,020
, Catharine,022
, Catherine(Mrs),054
, David,022
, E.H.(Mrs),054
, E.H.,054
, Elizabeth,045 ,058
, Eugene,020 ,048,049
, Eugine,050
, Frederick S.,046
, Hannah,037 ,047
, Harriet C.,019
, Henrietta C.,019,038,048
, J.L.(Mr.&Mrs),055
, J.L.(Mrs),056
, J.W.,019,021,023,024,046
, James H.,054
, James W.,023,024,047,056
, James,015 ,017,020,048,
049,061,064
, Jams,050
, Jamy,018,023
, John P.,050,052,054
, John T.,022
, John,041,050,052,054,057
, Joseph,037 ,047
, Julia Ann,041
, Lewis S.,022
, M.C.(Mrs),021
, M.C.,021
, Martha C.(Houck),018
, Martha C.,018 ,019,023,
037,046,048,050
, Martha S.,021 ,024
, Martha,023 ,024
, Mary E.,048,053
, Mary Eve,020
, Mary(Mrs Jno.),054
, Mattie C.,052
, Mattie S.,054
, Mattie,050
, W.E.,019,048,050
, William E.,023 ,038
, Wm.E.,019

BARBOUR, (Miss),044
, Catherine,008
, Christina,007
, David,011
, Elisabeth,009
, Geo.,008
, George,007,010,011
BARDALEBEN, Anne Margt.,009
, Arthur,009 ,010,012
, Harriet C.,009
, Margaret,009,010
, Mary,009,012
BARDELABEN, Arthur,006
, Margaret,006
, Wm.Arthur,006
BARGER, James W.,040,059
, Martha,040
BARNES, John,046
, Mary,046
BARSH, Anne,007
, Catharine,058
, Catherine,004,007,009
, Charlotte,004
, G.,093
, Geo.,091
, Geo.Henry,009
, Geo.Noah,010
, George,044 ,091
, Harriet,004
, John,004,007,009,043
BATES, Elizabeth,040
, R.W.(Dr),040
BECK, (Mr),086
, Jacob,077,079,081,083,084,
091,094
, Jaocb,092
, John Rudolph,006
, John,078
BENIGER, (Rev.),001
, Dorothy,039
BERLEY, W.(Rev.),003
BERNARD, D.(Rev),015
BERNHARD, D.,063,065,066
, David(Rev),031
, David,065
BERNHARDT, David(Rev),030
BERNHEIM, (Rev),002
BIRCHMORE, C.E.,019,021,048,050
, Charles E.,040
, Chas.W.J.,021
, Christiana E.,038
, Christiana,021
, Christianna,040
BLACKMAN, Charlotte,040
, David,040
BOND, Sarah,007
BONDS, Harriet R.,009
, Sarah,009
BOOKERT, ,066
, Henry(Dr),065
BOOKHARD, Elizabeth,059
, Henry,026
, Jane(Way),018
, John,026
, N.,015
BOOKHARDT, Eliz.,015
, Elizabeth,017,060
, Henry,060
, J.N.,017,059,060,065
, Jane,036
, John A.,015
, John,015,017,060,064,
065
, Mary,015,017,060
, Nicholas,065
BOOKHART, Elizabeth,022
, France E.,022
, J.M.,022
, Jane Eliz.,014
, Jas.Alexr.,014
, Jno.Nicholas,014
, Joel F.,022
, John N.,022

BORMIA(?), John,093
BOSCHARD, Susanna,057
BOSHATT, Wm.,005
BOSHETT, Anne Rebecca,009
, Elisa,005
, William,009
BOSTIC, Adeline,040
, William,040
BOUZARD, Albertos(Mr.&Mrs),055
, Lewis Daniel,055
BOWEN, Nathaniel(Rev),112
, Nathaniel,104,113
BOYD, R.J.,036
BRADDUM, Lawrence,040
, Mary,040
BRADEBURG, Magdelen,040
BRADENBURGH, Adeline,036
BRADHAM, Lawrence,018 ,019,023,
037
, Mary Ann,018
, Mary,023
, William Henry,023
BRANDBURG, James Martin,010
BRANDE, Magdelen,034
BRANDEBURG, Adam,010,011,012,034
,035,039
, Alexander,012
, Barbara,014
, C.,007
, Cath.,009 ,011
, Catherine,012 ,039
, Conrad,007 ,043
, David,010
, E.,047
, Eliza,041
, Jacob,005
, James,043
, Jas.William,047
, John Martin,011
, John,009,011,039
, Ludwig,010
, M.,008
, Margaret,039
, Marni,007
, Martin,005 ,007,009,
010,011,012,034,039,
044
, Mary E.,012
, Mary,040
, P.,047
, Rebecca,011
, Rosina,008 ,011,039
, Shadrack,011
, Sophia,010 ,011,012,
035,039
, T.Percy,041
BRANDENBERG, P.,064
, Perry,064
BRANDENBURG, Adeline,018
, Adline C.,021
, Connie,054
, E.C.(Mrs),051
, Effe B.,047
, Eliza C.,019 ,048,
050
, Eliza,021
, Harry C.,020
, Harvey C.,051 ,054
, James R.,021 ,054
, James W.,054
, James,025 ,062
, Jas.R.,020
, Jas.W.,020
, John K.,020,054
, John(Mrs),054
, John,021 ,026,041,
054
, Lizzie,056
BRANDENBURG, M.E.,021
, Martha E.,050
, Minnie A.,020 ,054
, Minnie,055
, Perry T.,050

```
              , Perry(Mrs),054         BUZHARD, (Son of Fred),054            , Henry I.,038
              , Perry,026              BUZHARDT, Fred(Mrs),054               , Henry J.,052
              , Silas,056              CALDWELL, (Mr),075 ,076,077           , J.J.,045
              , T.F.,048                       , Eva Ann(C),064              , J.P.,055
              , T.P.,051 ,053                  , J.M.,098 ,102,105,107       , Mary Ellen,041
              , T.Perry,021                    , Jno.,080                    , Minnie,055
BRANDENBURGH, Connie,020                       , Jno.M.,099,100,106   DARBY, A.T.(Dr),120
              , Effie,020                      , Jno.W.,097                  , N.T.,119
BRANDYBURG, ,066                               , John Jr.,086         DASH, Elisabeth,040
BRANDYBURGH, Adam,057                          , John,071 ,073,074,077,      , Elizabeth,011
              , Barbary,059                      082,083,085,086            , Geo.,011
              , John,057                       , Robert,101                 , John,044
              , Rebaca,059                     , Robt.,099,100,102,106, DASOR, Frederick(Rev),028
              , Rosana,057                       107                  DAVIS, (Mrs),083,084
              , Rosannah,058                   , Wm.(Mr),105                 , Eliza,081
              , Sophia,057                     , Wm.,097 ,099,100,101        , Elizabeth,078,079
BROWN, Gaspar,085                      CALER, (Mr),015                       , John,089
BUCHARD, (Mrs),034                     CALOR, Rachel,015               DE BARDALEBEN, Jennet,012
              , Henry,034 ,040,057     CAMPBELL, ,089                                , Louisa,010
              , John,010 ,034,057              , Eliza Rebecca,004     DE BARDELEBEN, Arthur,005
              , Magdalene,057                  , George Arnold,004                  , Elisabeth,034,039
              , Magdelen,035 ,040              , George,004                         , Henry,034
              , Mary Magdalen,010 ,011         , J.M.,097                           , John Fredrk.,005
              , Mary,058                       , James M.,094 ,096                  , Julianna,034
BUCHART, John,039                              , Mary Elisabeth,004                 , Margaret,005
BUCKINGHAM, Catharine,059              CAPSTEAD, Rebecca,011            DE LA VAUX, (Mr),105
              , Elias,082              CAR, Harrot,059                              , Francis,103
BULL, Capie D.,050 ,052                     , John,058                  DEATIN, W.A.(Rev),054
              , Dave,002               CARICK, (Mr),015                 DEBARDELEBEN, (Mr),089
              , Mary E.,038                   , Caroline,061             DELENY, Carolina Anne,010
              , Sarah,019,048,050             , Charlotte,061            DERRICK, (Rev),023 ,024,041
BURCHMORE, Mary Dorcas,010                                                      , (Rev.),019
              , Wm.Johnson,010         CARICK, Elizabeth,016                    , Amanda B.,001
BURDELL, John,081 ,082,083                  , Margaret,016                      , Henry David,001
BURK, Anne Christina,004               CARLE, Ephraim,035                       , John Edwin,001
              , Christina,004                , Jesse,035                        , P.(Rev),024
              , John Leoy,004                , Samuel,035                       , Paul(Rev),032 ,038,040
              , Laura,041                CARR, (Mrs),045                        , Paul(Rev.),001
BURKE, Amelia,047                             , Ann,018 ,036                    , Samuel H.,024
              , Clarissa,037                  , Eugena,040                      , Samuel Jos.H.,001
              , Sarah,037                     , Eugenia,017                     , Sidney Bartow,001
BURKET, (Miss),045                            , Henry,018,036,040,045,046, DREHER, Godfrey(Rev),029
              , (Widow),045                     047                       DREHR, Godfrey,026
              , ,061                          , Jennett,039               DUBOIS, Sam,087
              , Adam,016,040,045,058,060      , John Peter,046           DUFFORD, E.,023
              , Ann,016,017                   , Ugenia,018                DUPENT, Gideon,093
              , Barbara,061            CARSON, Caroline,040,046
              , Caroline,040                  , Gabriel,046               EADES, David,019,048
              , Casper,011 ,058,060    CATES, (Mrs),026                         , Mary A.,041
              , Elisabeth,017                , ,066                             , Mary Ann,019,024,038
              , Elizabeth,016 ,060           , C.,063 ,066                      , Rachael(col),050
              , Ellen,040                    , Catharine,061                    , Rachel,019 ,048
              , John Wm.,011                 , Charlotte,016             EASLER, Jacob,082
              , John,057                     , Christian,015,060         EBERHARD, Emeline,039
              , Lewis,016 ,060               , David,061                 EDES, Davis,021
              , Margaret,058                 , George,060                     , John David,021
              , Mary,045                     , Louisa,060                     , R.,021
              , Susanna,058,059              , Mary Ann,059              ELICK, Sarah(C),064
              , William,040                  , Mary,060,061              EMMIE, (Mrs.),043
BURKETT, (Miss),042                          , Polly,015                 ENTZMINGER, Eliz.,014
              , Adam,017 ,022                , Rosanna,015               ERWIN, James D.,040
              , Ann R.,022                   , Rossannah,060                   , Jas.David,013
              , Carolina,006           CAUFMAN, Ann(Mrs),053                    , Sarah Anne,013
              , Casper,006,009,012           , E.(Rev),053                      , Sarah F.,040
              , Elisabeth,009 ,034,039 CHEEVES, L.,119                          , Sarah Frances,013
              , Elizabeth,022 ,046     CLAREY, Joseph,079                ESLER, Jacob,081
              , John,006 ,042          CLARKE, Malcolm,082,085           EVANS, Elizabeth,040
              , Juliana,006            COBEL, Mary,013
              , Lewis,017 ,022,046     COBSTED, Jacob,059                EVANS, Rosa,055
              , Margaret,006           COLSEY, Charles,018,036                 , T.S.,055
              , Martha R.,022          CORBYN, Samuel,005                FARAR, Benj.,073,074,078,080
              , Mary,012 ,022          CORLEY, ,029                      FARRELL, James(Rev),090
              , Sophia,039             CORP, James,085                   FEARSHER, Christina,060
BUTLER, Geo.,110,111,117               CRABB, R.,097                     FELDER, (Miss),043
              , James,096              CUAGHMAN, Julia Ann,053                 , Abraham,008
BUTTLER, Adam,006                      CUBSTEAD, (Mrs.),044                    , Anne,004
              , Charles,005                     , Christopher,012              , Henry,004 ,006,007,008,
              , Chas.,005              CUMMINGS, B.,002                          043
              , Chas.Fredk.,009                 , Catherine,012                , Ludwig,006
              , Elisabeth,005                   , John,012                     , Margaret,006,007,039
              , George,004,006,009     DALLAS, J.,119                          , Margeret,004
              , James,004 ,005,008,011 DANSLER, John,044                       , Rebecca,007,008
              , John Patrick,011       DANTZLER, ,066                    FELKE, Mary,035
              , Ludwig,006                     , Ann,040                       , Melchoir,035
              , Mary,004 ,005,042              , Caroline E.,038         FELKEL, ,050,064
              , Thomas,005                     , David Anthony,052              , Abednego,010
              , William James,004              , F.Caroline,040                 , Ann Vernella,047
                                               , George,040                     , Anna J.,021
```

, Anna,054,055
, Baid,040
, Catherine E.,021
, Christianna,040
, Christina,023 ,026,059
, Derril,018 ,037
, Eliz.C.,052
, Elizabeth C.,050
, Ellen(Mrs),054
, Emma J.,019,038,048
, Eva,054,055
, Fannie C.,048
, Fanny C.,019,038
, Gabriel,040
, Herbert Luther,052
, Herbert,056
, J.A.,021
, J.K.(Mrs),054
, J.K.,021,047,051,052
, Jacob D.,021,050,052
, Jacob,054
, James,018 ,037
, Jo.Jr.,054
, Jo.K.,054
, John A.,038,050
, John C.C.,023
, John,018,019,037,054
, Jos.K.,048 ,049,050
, Jos.William,051
, Joseph K.,020 ,051
, Joseph,023
, Julia,056
, Lizzie,054
, Louisa,040
, M.A.(Mrs),021
, M.A.,021,047
, M.C.,052
, Martha Eva,051
, Martha Jane,040
, Mary A.,051
, Mary Ann,019,048,050,051
, Mary,058
, Nelie(Miss),050
, Rosa,021
, Thomas Milton,021
, Thomas,050 ,052
FELKLE, (Mast.),044
, Cath.Charlotte,011
, Catherine,034
, Christina,057
, Jacob,034
, John,035
, Mary,014
, Melchior,011,012,044,058
FERSNER, Ann Amelia,023
, Christena,015
, Christiana,022
, Cornelia E.,022
, Cornelia,041
, David,022 ,023,025,046
, Elizabeth A.,016
, Elizabeth,022 ,023,046
, Henry Joseph,046
, Jane,040
, Joseph,022
, Julia E.,022
FICHTER, Bastian(Mrs),042
FIELDER, Henry Sr.,085
FISHER, Charlotte S.,012
, Charlotte,012
, John,012,078
FITZPATRICK, John David,006
, Rebecca,039
, Rosina,006
FLIEGEL, Melchior,043
FLOOD, Jane,057
, Joseph,057
, Wm.,071 ,073,079
FOGEL, (Mrs),034
, Anne Harriet,012
, Anthony,004 ,057
, Catherine,039
, Charlotte,012
, Daniel,012 ,034,039,057
, Elisa,009
, Eliza S.,036
, Emanuel,036

, Harriet,007
, Jacob,010
, John,008,009,010,012,034,
  039,057
, Magdalen,009,012
, Magdelen,039
, Margaret,009,058
, Mary,058
, Peter,004
, Polly,058
, Rachel,007 ,039
, Samuel(Mast.),042
, Susanna,008
, William,044
FOGLE, David,018
, Eliza,017
FOGLE, Elizabeth,015,017,060
, Emanuel,018
, Mary Ann,016,061
, Peter,015,017,059,060
FOULER, Walace(C),064
FRANCKLOW, (Rev.),042 ,043
, Deborah Leah,001
, J.P. (Rev.),002
, John H.,044 ,034
, John Hepworth,001
, John P.(Rev.),001
, John Phillip,001
, Mary,040
, Rachell Anne,001
, Sarah F.,034,039
, Sarah Frances,001
, Sarah,001
FRANKLOW, (Rev)029,040
, ,029
, Deborah L.,034
, John P.(Rev),028
FRIEDERIAHS, John G.(Rev),027
  028
FRIERSON, Philip,084
, Phillip,088 ,089
FROELICH, John,039
, Leah,039
FROMM, (Mrs.),043
FRYERSON, Phil,079 ,080
GABEL, Mary Anne,012
GAEBEL, Christian,035
, Frederick,035
, Valentine,035
GAEBELIN, Eve,035
GAILLORD, (Capt),086
, Isaac,080,082,085,086
, Tac.,079
, Tacil.,086
, Tacilus,085
, Tacitus,071 ,073,074,
  075
GAITS, Ann M.,002
, Christian,057
, Conrad,002 ,057
, Elizabeth,002,057
, Frederick,057
, Harriot,002
, Jacob,057
, John D.,057
, John M.,002
, Joseph,002 ,058
, Lewis,002,058
, Magdalene,057
, Mary,057,058
, Samuel,058
, William,057
GARICK, Adam G.,022
, Adam Jr.,017,058
, Adam Sr.,045
, Adam,006,008,010,022,057
, Anne E.,012
, Anne Eliza,012
, Anne W.,035
, Anne,012,034,039
, Barbara,057
, Caroline,040
, Cath.,008
, Catharine,017
, Catherine,006 ,010,011,
  012,022,039
, Daniel,034 ,057
, David B.,017,036,050

, David,006 ,026,054,058
, Ellen,017
, Eve,007
, George,012 ,017,036,039,
  046,057
, Henry,017 ,023,036,040,
  057
, Jacob,040 ,057
, James Peter,023
, John J.,034
, John,006,007,008,010,011
  ,012,039,057
, Jos.,017
, Joseph,036
, Magdelen,012,040
, Magdelene,057
, Margaret,017,034,039,046
  ,057
, Maria,008
, Martin,017 ,018,062
, Mary Margt.,013
, Mary,023,034,057
, Patrick,011
, Peter,006
, R.A.,046
, Samuel,034 ,057
, Sophia,017 ,034,058
, William,012,013,017,057
, Wm.,026
GARLICK, Nancy,045
, William,045
GARRICK, Anne,039
, William,034,039
GATES, (Ch.?),019
, (Mast.),044
, (Miss),044
, (Mrs.),044
, Aaron G.,047,056
, Aaron,018,036,040,059
, Adam,011
, Alice M.,019,041,048
, Ann Caughman,047
, Anna Julia,051
, Anne Mary,039
, Bachman W.,019 ,038
, Bachmon W.,050
, Backman W.,048
, Barba E.,018
, Barbara E.,019
, C.,062
, C.Louisa,018,019
GATES, Catherine,002,009
, Charlotte L.,017
, Charlotte,014,034,039
, Chn.,008
, Christian A.,047
, Christian(Mrs),044
, Christian,001,006,009,011
  ,013,017,018,026,036
  ,039,062
, Conrad,004 ,006,009,011,
  013
, Daisy Rebecca,051
, Daniel,035
, David,005
, E.,052
, E.Louisa,048
, Eleanor E.,013
, Eleanora,044
, Elisabeth M.,011
, Elisebeth Margt.,002
, Elisabeth,001,004,006,011
  ,013,039
, Elison,038 ,040
, Elizabeth,034
, Ellison W.L.,022
, Ellison,019 ,048,050
, Eugena,016 ,040
, Eve Elisa,011
, Eve Matilda,010
, F.I.,019,021,026,047,048,
  049,050,051,052,053,
  054
, F.J.,052
, Frederick I.,021,041
, Frederick M.,021
, Frederick,010,011,013,019
  ,039

, Fredk.,011
, Fredk.Mortimer,047
, Geo.,001
, Geo.David,014
, Geo.Emanuel,051 ,053
, George,019 ,022,038,043
, Godfrey,013
, Gussie,050
, Harriet,009
, Jacob,010
, James Russell,013
, Jas.Russell,044
, Jas.Russell,014
, Jeff D.,054
, Jefferson A.D.,021
, Jefferson,019
, Jeffie A.D.,050
, Jeremiah,016,017,018
, John Christian,002 ,013
, John David,004
, John Martin,004 ,011
, John,011,013,020
, Joseph,006
, Julia Ann,053
, Lewis L.,014
, Lizzie St.Clair,052
, Lizzie,051
, Louisa,022
, Ludwig,004
, M.,066
, M.E.,021,047
, M.Julia Ann,018 ,019,048
, Magdalen,013
, Magdelen,011
, Mamie Etta,051
, Maria,006
, Martin,004 ,010,034,043
, Mary August,021
, Mary C.,039
, Mary E.,021 ,051
, Mary Ella,021,051
, Mary Ellen,019 ,038,041,
    048,053
, Mary Julia Ann,017
, Mary Julian,040
, Mary Maria,011
, Mary(Polly),053
, Mary,002,008,043
, Olivia,019 ,038
, P.,064
, Polly,017,018,019,048
, Rebecca,040
, Rosanna,017
, Rosina,010 ,011,013,039
, Rossanna,018
, Samuel,002 ,006
, Thos.Summers,052
, Valentine,006
, Verner Purcy,047
, William,001 ,011,035
, Wm.,014
GEISSENDANNER, John(Rev),027
GENOBLE, Anna,006
    , Elisa,008
    , John Adam,007
    , John,007 ,008
    , M.,008
    , Margaret,007 ,039
    , Sarah,005
GERELLS, Charles,040
    , Mary Ann,040
GIBBS, Mary,043
    , William,043
GIEGER, Jacob,035
GILBERT, Catherine,012 ,039
    , David,012 ,039
    , Robert Crabb,012
GLOECKLE, Anne,035
    , David,035
GOLDING, Geo.I.(?),054
BOLSON, Lewis,084 ,085
GOODMAN, (Mr),012
GOODWIN, Ann Elisa,012
    , Maddison,012
GOODWYN, (Dr.),046
    , J.W.,097
GOODWYN, Jno.W.,097
    , Martha,107

, R.H.(Col),118
, R.H.(Dr),113 ,116
, R.H.,108 ,109,110,115,
    119,120
, Robt. H.,114
, Robt.H.(Dr),110,111,115
, Robt.H.,107,113,117
, T.J.(Dr),120
, T.J.,119
, Thos.J.(Dr),110,111
, Thos.J.,117
, Wm.A.,115
GORDAN, ,103
GRAY, (General),012
, Mary,012

HABERMAN, Margaret,039
HAGLER, (Mr),100
HAIGLER, (Mast.),044
    , (Miss),044
    , (Mrs),044
, A.,013,062
, Adam,010 ,011,016,045,
    057,060,062
, Adriana C.,022
, Adriana,019
, Andrew,010
, Ann C.,037
, Ann Jane,016 ,017,018,
    019
, Ann,016,060
, Anna Jane,048
, Anna S.,040
, Anne,034
, C.,024
, Caroline F.,036
, Caroline,022 ,023
, Carrie M.,040
, Carrie,054,056
, Cary,024
, Catharine(Mrs),045
, Catherine,057 ,060
, Catherine C.,013
, Catherine,015 ,040
, Charlotte,014
, Clarence H.,023
, D.S.,040
, E.N.,024
, Edward P.,038
, Eleanora L.,012
, Elisabeth S.,047
, Elizabeth A.,061
, Elizabeth H.,060
, Elizabeth S.,017 ,018,
    060
, Elizabeth,016 ,022,023,
    058
, Ellen E.,038 ,040
, Emily,040
, Esau N.,040
, F.Caroline,040
, F.G.,050
, Fannie E.(Mrs),054
, Francis M.,022
, Frank,020 ,054
, Franklin,041
, Frederick,010
, G.R.(Rev),032
, G.R.,032
, Geo.R.(Rev),023,025,040
    ,047,063
, George F.G.,023
, George R.(Rev),037
, George R.,022
, George,015,023,061
, Georgiana,019 ,048
, Georgianna,038
, Georgina,023
, H.A.,025 ,056
, Henry A.,016 ,017,018,
    058,060
, Henry Aaron,047
, Henry E.,019 ,037
, Henry,006 ,008,010,011,
    012,039,060
, Hy,013
, J.Adam,026
, J.H.,045 ,064,065

, J.Henry,057
, Jacob,011
, James C.,040
, James,015 ,058,061
, Jane,040
, Jeremiah M.,011
, Jesse N.,015 ,022,025,
    040,060
, Jesse Nuel,013
, Jesse,023
, Jn.,060
, Jn.Henry,026
, John A.,057,060
, John H.,015
, John James,006
, John L.,015,022
, John Peter,016,023
, John,016 ,017,026,057
, Joseph,064
, Joshua,016,025,059,060
, Josiah E.,024
, Josiah,010 ,060
, Julia,055
, Laura,041 ,050
, Lewis,023 ,026,058,060,
    062
, Lula,056
, Luther W.,022
, Margaret,016 ,022,023,
    036
, Martha,019,038
, Mary Agnes,024
, Mary B.,016,022
HAIGLER, Mary C.,014
, Mary Charlotte,014
, Mary M.(Houck),018
, Mary M.,018,037
, Mary,006 ,020,023,026,
    061
, N.P.,022 ,059
, N.Patrick,017
, P.,064
, Patrick,011,015,023,059
    ,060,065
, Peter,058 ,060
, Rosina,013,034
, Sarah M.,016 ,061
, Sarah,018 ,019,037,041
, Seleana,059
, Shadrach S.,011
, T.S.(Mr.&Mrs),055
, T.S.,054
, Thos.Shadrach,055
, William L.,022
, William,041
HAILES, Geo.,082,085
HAILS, Geo.,082
, Robt.(Capt),088 ,096
, Robt.,089,090,094,097
HAIR, (Child),015
, Adam,034 ,057
, Catharine,058
, Charlotte,043
, Conrad,005,006,042
, Daniel,034,061
, David,008,009,044
, Eleanora C.,008
, Elisabeth,006,039
, J.,008
, Jacob Edmond,012
, Jacob Henry,013
, Jacob,009,044
, James Ludwig,011
, James,007,009,011,012,013,
    039,057
, John,009 ,043
, Lewis,036
, Magdelen,012 ,034,040
, Margaret,005 ,008,011,013,
    016,017,026,039,057
, Martin,006
, Mary,007 ,015,017,060
, Peter(Mrs),034
, Peter,008
, Rosina Cath.,006
, Sophia,035,057
, William,005

HALES, Robt.,090
   , Thos.,078
HALLMAN, (?),048
   , (Rev),020
   , Milledge S.,002,052
   , S.T.(Rev),047 ,051
   , S.T.(Rev.),002
   , Sarah Jane,002
HALTIWANGER, Geo.Sr.(Rev),030
HANE, J.K.,071
HAPPOLDT, Emma,041
HARDWICK, Margaret,039
   , Richard,039
HARMAN, Catharine,061
   , Catherine,016
   , Jacob,014 ,015,019
   , John C.,019,038
   , John Calvin,014
   , Katherine,014
   , Magdalen,006
   , Mary,016,019
   , Phillip(Mrs),042
HARMON, J.(?) Jr.,019
   , J.W.,047
   , Jacob,017 ,018,046,048,
        053,060
   , John C.,048,050,053
   , Mary,017,018,046,048,053
        ,060
   , Melchior A.,046
   , Philip,006
HARRIS, Amos,039
   , Anne,039
HART, Benjamin,005
   , Derril(Maj),088
   , Emma Cassia,005
HASKELE, E.(Maj),105,108
HASKELL, C.(Mrs),119,120
   , Chas.T.,115
   , W.E.,119 ,120
   , Wm.E.,118
HASLUM, Margaret,026,039
   , Mary,039
   , Thomas,039
   , William,039
HAUCK, (Miss),039
HAWKINS, (Dr),026
   , (Mrs),003
   , ,031
   , Charles Duval,003
   , Emma Kinard,003
   , Helen Rude,003
   , J.(Rev.),003
   , J.W.Selers,003
   , Jacob(Rev.),001
   , Jennie,054
   , John Jacob,003
   , John,071
   , Joseph Wingard,003
   , Mary Ella,003
   , Mary,003
   , Peter H.(Rev.),003
   , Sarah Elizabeth,003
   , T.(Rev),020,026
   , T.(Rev.?),047
   , Virginia,003
   , Willie Scherimer,003
   , Willie Schirmer,003
HAZELIUS, (Rev),028
HEALTHY, Chas.,087
HEALY, Wm.,074
HEAPE, James,055
HEATLY, (Col),095 ,099,102
   , A.(Col),103,105
   , A.,097
   , Andrew(Col),104
   , Andrew,094 ,095,096,097,
        099,100,101,103,105,
        107,108
   , Andrw,099
   , Chas.,079 ,082,085,087
   , William,002
   , Wm. Jr.(Capt),088
   , Wm.,071,073,075,078,080,
        089,090,091,092,093,
        094,095
HECKELL, Catherine,039
   , Frederick,042

HENDRIC, Ann C.,017
   , S.Thos.,017
HENDRIX, ,029
HENKEL, David(Rev),057
HENKLE, David(Rev),029
HERMAN, John,005
   , Philip,005
HERRICK, Barbara,060
HERROD, Jesse(C),066
HERSHER, Samuel(Rev),029
HESSE, William,004
HILL, Wm.,081
HILLER, Amanda B.,001
   , Martha,012
HOBER, Jacob,057
   , Jon,057
HOBERMAN, Mary,057
HOFFMAN, ,006
   , Andrew,057
   , Ann Eliza,058
   , Anne Rebecca,012
   , Barbara,005,006,013,044
   , Barbary,026
   , Catherine,008
   , Daniel,060
   , Danniel,005
   , E.,008
   , Eleanora E.,013
   , Elisabeth,006 ,008,039
   , Elizabeth,034 ,039
   , George,009
   , Jacob,039
   , John A.,007,009,057
   , John Andrew,005
   , John,005 ,006,008,012,
        039,042,043
   , Joseph,013
   , Lewis,057 ,061
   , Ludwig,035
   , Mary B.,057,060
   , Mary Elisabeth,004
   , Mary Jocobina,043
   , Mary,005 ,007,009,012,
        057
   , Melchior,034 ,042
   , Rebecca,006
   , Rosanna,026
   , Rosannah,060
   , Sophia,039
   , Wm.Robert,007 ,042
   , Wm.Robt.,008
HOFMAN, Andrew,035
HOLLAND, Y.(Rev.),003
HOLLOWAY, Corrie E.,050,051
   , J.B.O.,051
   , Maggie O'Neall,051
HOLMAN, Mrs.),043
   , ,066,071
   , A.(Maj),055
   , A.D.,024
   , Adam Melchior,007
   , Adam,024,062
   , Alfred W.,052
   , Ann C.,052
   , Ann Caroline,021
   , Ann Catherine,001 ,013
   , Anna C.,050
   , Anne,039
   , Benj.Melchior,047
   , Brandeburg, J.,062
   , Catharine,061
   , Charles(Mast.),042
   , Conrad,011 ,039,093,097
   , Corrie E.,048
   , Corrie,020 ,038
   , David Luther,001,013,044
   , E.,021 ,024,047
   , Ed,055
   , Elisabeth,034
   , Eliz.Rachel,013
   , Elizabeth Rachel,001
   , Emma L.,052
   , Emma Louise,055
   , Emma(Mrs),054
   , Emma,019,021,038,040,048
        ,050,051
   , Est.,062
   , Eugenah Rebaca,001

   , Eugenia Rebaca,013
   , Eugenia,043
   , Eugina,005
   , Eve Mary,001,012,044
   , Fannie E.,050 ,052
   , G.B.(Mrs),054
   , G.B.,050
   , Geo.Edward,051
   , George,020
   , Gussie B.,050
   , Gussie b.,052
   , Heford,056
   , J.,064
   , J.C.,065
   , J.K.,062
   , J.M.,054
HOLMAN, James Moss,021
   , James T.,015
   , James Thomas,001
   , Jas.M.,020
   , Jas.Thos.,013
   , Jesse Knodle,013
   , Jesse,062
   , Jessey Knodel,001
   , Jn.C.,026 ,060
   , John C.,013,015,057,065,
        066
   , John Conrad,001,012,013
   , John Jos.,013
   , John Joseph,001
   , John R.,013
   , John Russell,001,044
   , John,025,054
   , Joseph,039 ,042
   , Lovey(C),064
   , M.K.(Dr),019,020,021,026
        ,040,048,049,050,051
        ,052,054
   , M.K.(Dr.),047
   , M.K.,021,047
   , M.Kennerly,024
   , March(C),064
   , Margaret A.(Mrs),054
   , Margaret A.,019,038,048,
        050
   , Mary Jane,020 ,051,054
   , Mary,005,007,008
   , Melcher,094
   , Melchior,007,008,043
   , Melchoir,005
   , Melchor,095,096
   , Milledge S.,050
   , Osgood,050 ,052,054
   , Rachel,013 ,015,057,060
   , Rachell,001,011,012,013,
        035,039
   , Salena Cath.,047
   , T.,066
   , T.K.,063
   , Thomas,034
   , W.M.(Mr.&Mrs),055
   , W.M.,054
   , William Conrad,001
   , Wm.C.,015 ,059,060
   , Wm.Conrad,011
HOOVER, Adison(C),064
   , Ann,018
HOPE, J.C.,028
   , John C.(Rev),030
HOUCK, Ann,016 ,017
   , Anne,039
   , Casper,039
   , Henry,026,060
   , Jacob P.,023,024
   , Jacob Patrick,021
   , John,042
   , M.(Mrs),021
   , Magdelen,040
   , Mary M.,019 ,048
   , Mary,023
   , W.(Rev),023
   , W.A.(Rev),021
   , William,018
   , Willie,052
   , Wm.,018
   , Wm.D.,023
   , Wm.Derrick,021

HOUGH, G.A.,020,048,049
 , Geo.A.(Rev),049
 , Geo.A.(Rev.),002
 , Sallie M.,002
 , Willie Rude,002
HOUK, Henry,016
HOUSER, (Mr),042
 , (Mrs),042
 , Ann,017,022,036,046
 , C.,006
 , Cath.Susanna,013
 , Christina,039
 , D.S.,046
 , Derril1,022
 , E.,008
 , Elisabeth Cath.,006
 , Elisabeth,013
 , Elizabeth,039
 , Jacob,008 ,013,039
 , Magdelen,039
 , Mary Eliz.A.,022
 , Mary,039
 , Paul Jefferson,046
 , Rachell,044
 , Reuben Christ.,008
 , Reuben(Mast.),043
HRABOWSKI, Ann,110 ,111
 , T.T.,109
 , Thos T.,111
 , Thos.,108
 , Thos.T.,110 ,115
HUBER, Anne,039,044
 , E.Anne,044
 , Elisabeth E.,008
 , Elisabeth,008,043
 , Jacob,007,008,039
 , John,043
 , Magdelen,039
 , Richard Henry,007
HUBLER, Samuel,016
HUFFMAN, Ann E.C.,014
 , Daniel,014,015,017,022
 , Elisabeth Garick,018
 , Ellen,016 ,040
 , K.,014
 , Lewis,017 ,019,047
 , Luther E.,022
 , Mary Ann,036 ,040
 , Mary B.,016,017
 , Mary,015 ,017,018,036
 , Melchoir,018
 , Melchor,037
HUFFMAN, Rosanna,016,017,022
 , Selena,018,037
 , Susan Eliz.,014
 , Susanna,036
 , Susannah,017
HUNGEPELER, Mary,016
HUNGEPELAR, Mary,060
HUNGEPEALER, D.,060
 , Elizabeth,017
 , John,017
 , Lewis,018
 , Russel,017
HUNGEPEILER, Mary,018
HUNGEPELER, David(Rev),031
 , Eliz.,016
 , Elizabeth,019 ,061
 , Louisa,016,061
 , Mary,017
HUNGERPIELAR, Louisa,040
 , Russel,036
HUNGERPIELER, Carrie M.,040
 , Elisabeth,018
 , Lewis,018,036
 , Margaret,040
 , Mary Jr.,018 ,037
 , Mary,047
 , Russel,018
 , Scheck,018
 , Schwartz,018
 , Sheck,018
HUNKELPEELER, (Mrs.),043
HYDES, (Mr),081
HYDRICK, Gideon E.,037
INABINET, ,062
INNEGER, Elisabeth,013

IRICK, (Mr),100,102
 , Alice M.,041
 , Alice(Mrs),049
 , Anne Mary,039
 , Catharine,060
 , Catharinee,022
 , Charlotte L.,010
 , Chas.Richardson,014
 , Edinborough F.,022
 , Edwina Maria,022
 , Elisa,018
 , Elisabeth,018,034,034
 , Eliz.Margt.,014
 , Eliza,014,015,017,022,061
 , Elizabeth,016,017,023,047
 , George,023 ,047
 , Hariot,058
 , Harriet,034
 , I.Martin,056
 , J.M.,018,019,048,059
 , J.M.Sr.,017
 , J.Martin,047
 , J.Valentine,045
 , James M.,014
 , James Morgan,061
 , Joel Adams,023
 , John A.,014 ,015
 , John Alexr.,008
 , John M.,022 ,060
 , John Martin,014
 , Julia Ann,016
 , Julian,061
 , Labon,041
 , Margaret,034,039
 , Marla,035
 , Martin Sr.,065
 , Martin,014 ,034,044,057
 , Mary Ann,016 ,036
 , Mary Julian,040
 , Mary Martha,009
 , Mary T.,016
 , Mary,009,010,011,012,015,
   017,035,040,045,058,
   060,061
 , Morgan,011
 , Rebaca,059
 , Robert Jr.,018 ,019,037
 , Robert,060
 , Rosina,039
 , Sophia,043
 , Valentine,008,009,010,011
   ,012,016,026,039,045
   ,057,060
 , W.R.,022
 , Wm.Martin,014
 , Wm.Robert,006
JACKSON, Barbara E.,019
 , Barbara(Mrs),049
 , Catherine,086
 , David,045 ,081,083
 , Edward,039
 , Laval,036
 , Mary Ann,015 ,061
 , Mary,015 ,017,061
 , Rebecca,039
 , Rosanna,015,017,061
 , Sarah,018
JENKINS, Edward(Rev),098
JOHNSON, Richard(Rev),118
 , Samuel,018
JOHNSTON, Lewis,036
 , Samuel,036
JONES, (Mr),093
 , Capers,040
 , Ellen E.,040
 , Henry(Mr.&Mrs),055
 , Henry(Mrs),054
 , Herman Hawkins,055
 , J.I.(Mr.&Mrs.),055
 , Jane(Mrs),053
 , Lewis(Mrs),054
 , Walter Wolfe,055
 , Wolfe,055
JOSEPH, Harriet(C),064
JOYNER, Ann,039
 , Daniel,039
 , Exekiel,039
 , Margaret,039

JUENIGER, John,035
JUNERSON, V.(Dr),111
 , V.D.(Dr),110
KAEMERLAERDER, Daniel,035
KARICK, Adam Jr.,015
 , Ann,016
 , Caroline,016
 , Catherine,016
 , Chas.David,014
 , Daniel Jos.,014
 , Derril Shadrick,014
 , Geo.Wm.,014
 , George,034
 , John Martin,014
 , Martin,015
 , Mary Eliz.,014
 , Wm.,014,015,060
KARRICK, Ann,060
 , Daniel,014
 , David B.,014
 , Mary Magdelene,014
 , William,014
KAVICK, Catharine,060
KEEBLER, Samuel,061
KEGLER, Anne,013
 , John,013
 , Mary,013
KEITT, Emmaly V.,041
 , George,025
 , John D.,040
 , Mary Ann,040
 , Texas,040
KEITTS, ,064
 , G.,062 ,063,064
KELLAR, Catharine,058 ,060
 , Eliza,058
 , Frederick,058
 , J.J.,060
 , Jacob,057 ,058,060
 , Magdelene,060
 , Rebacak,060
 , Rosanna,058
 , Susannah,060
 , Susanna,057
KELLARS, R.W.,064
KELLER, (Dr),049,064
 , (Mrs.),043
 , ,066
 , A.,047
 , Aaron,018
 , Alice M.,038
 , Ann,019,021,023,040,048,
   050
 , Anne,034
 , Aron,004
 , Catharine,015 ,019,062
 , Catherine C.,013
 , Catherine,017 ,018,048,
   050
 , Charles,047
 , Christina,007 ,011,024,
   039
 , Clarance,046
 , Conrad,044
 , Elisabeth,011 ,044
 , Eliza,041 ,046
 , Elizabeth E.,019,048,050
 , Ellen,016
 , F.E.(Mrs),054
 , Fannie E.,050
 , Frances E.,048
 , Frances,019,046
 , Francy,018
 , Frederick,044
 , Ida C.,019 ,038,048
 , J.A.(Dr),019,048,053
 , J.Jacob,026
 , J.W.,022
 , Jacob,002 ,004,006,007,
   011,015,018,026,036,
   039,045
 , James D.,026
 , Jane,018,037
 , Jas.Aiken,050 ,052
 , Jefferson M.,019
 , John J.,105
 , John Lewis,022
 , John Sr.,037

, John W.,015,017
, John,002,013,035,042,045
  ,058
, Jos.David,010 ,044
, Joseph A.,018 ,037
, Joseph,015 ,034,044
, Lewis,018 ,036
, Lovey,018 ,037
, M.E.,041
, Magdalen,016
, Magdeline(Mrs),045
, Margaret,013
, Maria,018 ,036
, Martha E.,019 ,038,048
, Martin Andrew,011
, Mary A.,038,047
, Mary Della,019
, Mary Frances,047
, Mary,013,045
, Morgan,046
, Philip,011 ,013
, R.W.,021,023,047
, Rachel,016 ,017,022,061
, Rosa C.,021,023
, Rosina,006 ,007
, Rupel,024
, Russel,018 ,019,037,046
, Susanah,017
, Susanna,006,007
, Susannah,015
, Sussanna,034
, W.,066
, W.R.,019,040,048,050
, William,042,046
, Wm.,061,063
KELLY, Alexander,081
, Daniel,089
, Simon,081
KEMMERLIN, Ann,041
, Daniel,057
, Elmore,055
, Jas.K.(Mrs),054
, Mary Ann,040
, Mary(Mrs),054
KENNERLY, (Mrs),025
, Anne,042
, J.,066
, J.C.,062
, Jn.,066
, Jn.C.,063
, John C.,066
, Rebecca,039
, Thomas,039
KERRICK, Adam Sr.,060
, Adam,060
, Barbara,060
, Daniel,061
, George,060
, John M.,060
, Mary,060 ,061
, Rebaca,061
, Sophia,016
, Sopphia,060
KIEBLER, Samuel,034
KIB(KEY), Dederick,045
KILLICK, George,094
KILLICKS, Geo.,095 ,096
KILLINGSWORTH, Eliza,014
KING, (Mrs),042
, Anna,037
, Catherine,039
, Christopher,004 ,007
, Elisabeth,004
, Ephraim(Mast.),042
, Ephraim,007
, Frederick,034
, Geo.,080 ,082,083,085,086,
  087
, Phillip,015
KINLEIN, Elisabeth,043
KISTLER, (Rev),023
KITT, Elizabeth,061
KITTS, (Mrs),015
, ,066
, G.,066
KLEIN, Rebecca,008
KOFFMAN, Barbara,034

KRAEMER, Anne,035
KUHN, Anne,039
KUMPF, (Mrs),042
LANE, Rollin,037
LAWTON, W.H.,066
LAYTIN, Jessie(Miss),054
, Lettie,054
, Minnie,054
, Zenith,054
LAYTON, Jesse,020
, R.D.,054
, Salina(Mrs),054
LEIGS, Mary,035
LENTZ, Theobald,044
LEPPARD, J.F.W.(Rev),032
LESSNE, Francis,090
LEVER, Elias,079,081
LEWIS, Rochsena(C),064
, Wm.,019,119
, Wm.L.(Capt),110 ,117
, Wm.L.,107,108,109,111,113
  ,114,115,116,117
LINTON, John,089
LITTLE, Aaron,087 ,088
LIVINGSTEN, Jno.,080
LIVINGSTON, Jane Sarah,009
, Jno.,008
, John,010,044
, Moses Robt.,006
, Samuel,010
, William,006
, Wm.,007,009,088
LIVISTEN, Jno.,080
, John Jr.,074
, John,075
, Wm.,082
LIVISTON, Wm.,081 ,083,084,086,
  087
LLOYD, John,071,073
LOISTON, John,072
LOVELL, (Mrs),117
, Ann(Mrs),110,111
, Ann,115,116
, J.(Mr),103
, James,090 ,099,100,101,
  102,103,107,108
LOVEL1, James,099
LOWMAN, Nancy,064
LOYD, Adam,034
, Elizabeth,058
LUEBRAND, Elisabeth,035
, Sarah,035
MACK, Eugenia,016,022
, Eugenia,017 ,022,046
, Harriet E.,022
, Harriet Eliza,046
, John,017 ,022,034,046
, Ludwig(Mast.),042
, Mary Jane,022
, Mary,039
MACKINY, Anne Christina,009
, Chas. Alexr.,009
, Elisabeth,009
MARGART, A.C.,022
, Ann Mary J.,022
, Franklin S.,022
, J.P.(Rev),023 ,030,040,
  045,046,062
, J.P.,017 ,022
, John P.,062,033
MARKLEY, Rosina,035
MCCLURE, D.(Capt),065
, D.C.,017
, David,015 ,061
, Jane,018 ,037
, Mary,016 ,017,060
MCCORD, Eliz.Mary,007
, J.R.,109
, Jno.T.,106 ,107
, John T.,101,107
, Jos.R.,107 ,108,109,110,
  111,113,116
, Joseph,007
, Mary,043
, R.P.,110,111
, Sophia Anne,007

MCGRILL, Charlotte,016 ,017,03(
, Eliza E.,014
, Eliza,018 ,036
, Emily,040
, John,014 ,039
, Richard,040
, Richd.Alexr.,014
, Samuel D.,014
, Sharlott,061
MCKINNEY, (Rev),118
MCMARLIN, Mordecai,078
MCMICHAEL, John(Mrs),054
MEAGLER, Conrad,058
, Elizabeth,060
, John,061
, Rachel,057
MEIGLER, Catherine,034 ,040
, Conrad,007,009
, Harriet,007
, Rebecca,009
MENICKEN, Elisabeth,039
, John A.,035 ,039
, John Anthony,002
MENIKEN, Eleanora,011
, Elisabeth,011
, John A.,011
MENNICKEN, Anthony,057
MENNICKENS, (Dr),099
MENNIKEN, Elisa Frederica,012
, Elisabeth,012
, John,012
MEYARS, Elizabeth,058
MEYERS, David,069
, Elisa,009
, Elisabeth,009 ,010
, John,010
, Juliiana M.M.,008
MIEGLER, Anne,043
, Cath.Lucretia,006
, Conrad,004,006
, Mary Magdalen,011
, Mary,004
, Peter(Mrs),042
MILES, J.T.,119
, James T.,109,110,113,117
, Jas.T.,109 ,110,111,113,
  114,115,116,117,118,
  120
MILLER, Elizabeth,039
, Robert,006
MINEGER, Elizabeth,016
MINNICKEN, Elizabeth,057
MINTZ, Frederick,012,042
, Jacob,043
, Margaret,042
, Maria,042
, William,012
MITCELL, John,074
MITCHEL, John,073 ,077
MITCHELL, Eliza,060
, John,071
MONK, John,087 ,098
MOORER, Anne,039
MOSS, Emma,040
MUERHOFFER, (Rev),029
MUETZIN, Catherine,035
MULENBURG, (Dr),027,028
MURDY, Charlotte,040
MURPH, Barbara,007 ,043
, Henry,039
, Jane,007,008,039
, John Henry,008
, Rosina,039
, Rudoff,043
, Rudolph,007 ,008,039
MURRAY, Jeter(Miss),055
MYDDLETEN, Chas.(Col),089
MYDDLETON, W.J.(Col),105
, W.J.,098,099,102,103
, Wm.J.,099,100,101,104
MYERS, David,005,008,012,039
, Elina Rebecca,013
, Elisabeth,012,039
, Eugena,040
, Eugenia,017
, John,043
, Joshua,012 ,040
, Kitts(C),066

```
             , Wm.George,005
MYRES, Emma,041
     , Judson J.,041
NEGRO, Adella,064
NEISLER, Daniel,035
       , Jn.(Mr),042
NICHAL, John M.,073
NICHOLS, John M.,074,075,078
NIXON, Alexr.Gillon,005
NOBLE, Jas.,120
NODLE, Rachell,039
OCANE, J.H.,055
OLIN, Winey(C),064
OLIVER, Ada,020,054
      , Georgia,050
      , W.W.(Mrs),050
      , W.W.,050,054
      , Willie,020
OLLIVER, Henry,005


OSMAN, Cath.Barbara,044
     , George,040
     , Margaret(Mrs),044
     , Maria Cath.,044
OTT, Josiah,041
   , Julia,041
PAILOR, Mary,036
PALMER, Jos.,087
      , Jos.Jr.,087
PARLER, Abednego,012,044
      , Anne,012,039
      , Elisabeth,016
      , Elizabeth,017
      , F.,052
      , Fanny(Mrs),054
      , J.,052
      , John Little,011
      , Maggie,056
      , Mary,018
      , Ozro Harman,052
      , Paul,054
      , Rosanna,016
      , Shadrach,011
PARLOR, Abednego,010
      , Ann E.,022
      , Ann R.,022
      , Elizabeth,022
      , Fannie C.,050
      , Mary E.J.,022
      , Mary,056
      , Pearl,020
      , Rachell anne,010
      , S.B.,022
PARLOUR, Rebecca Ann,014
PATERSON, Henry(C),064
PEIN, Adam,009
    , Catherine,010,042,043
    , Elisabeth,044
    , Elizabeth,005
    , Frederick,005,010
    , Fredk.,008,009
    , Jane(Miss),042
    , John,008 ,035,044
    , Magdelen,035
PERRIN, W.C.(Mrs),054
PIEGLER, Catherine,039
PIERCE, James,081
PINE, Barbara,058
    , Frederick,057
    , Jacob,057
    , Joseph,057
    , Mary,057
PLATT, Thos.,074,078
PLATTE, Thos.,075
PORTER, John,039
      , Margaret,039
POU, Gavin,073
POWEL, Jacob,039
PRICKET, Rebecca,040
PROBST, J.F.(Rev),051  ,052,053
PROTHRO, Adrianna S.,050
       , Emma Jane,053
       , Willie,050,052
PURCY, Verner,049

RANAH, (Rev),029
```

```
RANCH, David,013
     , Geo.Steven,013
     , M.(Rev),029
RAST, (Mrs),015
    , A.,015
    , A.M.,047
    , Adam,007  ,015,026,046,058,
                 060,065
    , Ann,058  ,060
    , Anna M.(Mrs),054
    , Anna M.,048  ,050
    , Anna,019 ,021,023,024,038
    , Anne Susanna,011
    , Annie M.Jr.,048  ,050
    , Annie,020,049
    , Barbara,004  ,007
    , C.,046
    , C.J.(Mr.&Mrs),055
    , Catharine,037
    , Catherine,002,034
    , Charlotte Eliz.,055
    , Charlotte,016,025
    , Christian,058
    , Christina,002
    , Claude J.,054
    , Claudius J.,021  ,023,024,
                  050,052
    , Conrad(Mast.),042
    , Conrad,004,008,009,010,011
                 ,013,026,057
    , David,005
    , E.G.,054
    , Earnest M.,050
    , Earnest Manly,047
    , Ed(Mr.&Mrs),055
    , Eddie Lon,055
    , Elisabeth,009,034
    , Eliza,009,016,060
    , Elizabeth,002,058,060
    , Ella May,055
    , Ernest M.,054
    , Eve,007
    , Frances E.,036
    , Frances,017
    , Frederick,004,005,058
    , Fredk.,008
    , G.D.,019 ,021,023,026,047,
                048,049,051
    , Geo.,015
    , Geo.Adam,050
    , Geo.D.,050,054
    , Geo.Edw.,052
    , Geo.Edward,050
    , George Adam,021
    , George D.,018,037
    , George E.,021,023,024
RAST, George,002,004,006,024,026
                 ,057,060
    , Gussie M.(Mrs),054
    , H.E.(Mr.&Mrs),055
    , H.E.(Mrs),056
    , Hannah,002,004,006,035,057
                 ,058,060
    , Harriet,046
    , Heber E.,054
    , Heber Elliott,047
    , Heber,050
    , Henry,008,046,058,060
    , J.L.,019 ,021,023,024,026,
                047,048
    , Jacob,045
    , James L.,054
    , James,019,024
    , Jas.L.,049,050
    , John A.,014
    , John Adam,002,006
    , John David,014,017
    , John Fredk.,008
    , John(Mast.),042
    , John,004 ,007,008
    , Joseph,004,022
    , Lectra Christena,046
    , Lena H.,050
    , Lena,052 ,054
    , Lula(Mrs),054
    , Luther,056
    , M.Charlotte,018
    , M.J.(Mrs),021
```

```
    , M.J.,021  ,047
    , Magdeline,002
    , Margaret Ann,021  ,023
    , Margaret Anna,024
    , Margaret(Mrs),055
    , Margaret,018 ,034,036,057
    , Margret,002
    , Mary Ann,037
    , Mary C.,060
    , Mary Charlotte,017
    , Mary J.(Mrs),053
    , Mary Jane,023,024,051
    , Mary Katherine,014
    , Mary Magdelen,013
    , Mary,002 ,004,016,022,034
                  057
    , Mathias,004  ,007,009
    , Mattie Ellen,055
    , Morgan,026,036,047
    , Novice Delura,021
    , Novice L.,047,050,052
    , Novice,026
    , Rosanna,058
    , Samuel D.M.,022
    , Samuel,008,022,061
    , T.O.(Miss),055
    , William,034  ,058
    , Willie A.,054
    , Willie Aiken,051
    , Willie,020
RAUCH, Anne,039
     , George S.,039
     , Luvera,058
     , Margaret,058
RAY, Margaret,039
RAYE, Eugenia,013
    , John,013
    , Magdelen,013
REICHARD, Barbara,043
REID, H.(Mrs),111
    , H.,110
    , Wm.,087
RICHARDSON, ,115
          , E.(Col),103,105
          , E.,119  ,120
          , Ed.(Col),110,111,11
                   ,115,116,117
          , Ed.,102,103,105,107
                   108,109,114
          , Edw.(Capt),088
          , Edw.,099,106,113
          , Edward,100 ,101,102
                    107
RICKENBACKER, (Mrs.),043
            , Belle,055
            , Cornelia,041
            , Elizar,041
            , Franklin,041
            , Henry L.,055
            , Henry,040,055
            , M.A.(Mrs),040
            , Thomas E.,041
RICKENBAKER, Anna,037
           , Caroline,037
           , Elizabeth,037
           , Henry L.,037
           , Jacob,037
           , Jane,037
           , Martha,037
           , Rachell,009
           , Samuel,037
RILEY, M.A.,040


RISER, Ann,061
    , Anna S.,040
    , Anne Sussana,006
    , Carrie,021
    , Elizabeth,058
    , George A.,040
    , Jacob,058
    , John,018,036
    , Joseph,005  ,006,018,036
                   058
    , Mary,017,058
    , Sarah,016,017
    , W.D.,021
    , Wilber L.H.,021
```

ROISER, Mary,015
ROOF, Hetty E.,041
, Simeon W.,041
ROSS, Elizabeth,016,017,060
, Jacob,060
ROUCHE, Francis,083
ROWE, Chas.,073
, Christopher,084 ,085
, Samuel,073
ROY, Anne,002
, Elisabeth,007
, Elizabeth,004 ,005,006
, Geo.,007
, George Russel,002
, George,004,005,006
, Jacob Martin,002 ,006
, James Drane,002
, John Aron,002 ,005,042
, John,040
, Magdelen,040
, Maria,002 ,004
, Pearce,007
, Perce,002
ROYE, Elisabeth,002
, George,002
RUCKETT, Jacob,035
RUFF, Mary,035
RUSH, Annie(Mrs),054
, Charles C.,058
, Charley,054
, Charlie,056
, Elizabeth,058
, George C.,039
, Harman,044
, Harmon,026,054
, Laurence N.,038
, Lawrence,054
, Mary Ann(Mrs),054
, Nina,054
, Paul D.,037
, Willie,020,054
RUSSELL, James,002
RUTLEDGE, J.(Mrs),120
RYER, Elisabeth,035
RYSER, (Mast.),044
, (Mrs),040
, Elizabeth,005
, Jacob,035
, Joseph,035 ,043
, Josiah,013
, Mary Ann,013
, Mary,035

SAAB, Thos.,080
SABB, (Col),096
, Amy(C),064
, Ann(C),064
, Jos.,087
, Morgan(Maj),088
, Morgan,082,089,090
, Sarah F.,040
, Sarah,039
, THos.,089
, Thomas Jr.,083,086
, Thomas(Col),088
, Thomas,039
, Thos Jr.,097
, Thos.(Col),092,093
, Thos.,071,073,087,089,093,
094,095,096,097
, Thos.Jr.,085 ,087
, Thos.,090
SAGER, William,008
SAUERHAFFEN, Conrad,039
, Elizabeth,039
SAUERHAFIN, Conrad,007
, Elizabeth,007
, Henry,007
SAVAGE, Chas.,082
, Jno.,086
, John,082,084,085,086
SCHAEFF, W.C.(Rev),030
SCHECK, John D.(Rev),065
, John D.,003
, Joicee C.,003
, Luther Whitfield,003
, Mary Ann Eliza,003
SCHIRMUS, Jacob F.,029
SCHNIDER, Elisabeth,035
, Jacob,035

SEAGLER, Jacob,058
, Margaret,058
SEGAR, John,011
, Sarah,011
SEGER, Catherine,004
, John,004,008
SELLARS, Andrew,005,057
, Daniel,057
, Elizabeth,057
, George,058
, John,005
, William,059
SELLERS, (Miss),043
, (Mrs),044
, A.,008
, Adriana(Mrs),054
, Adriana,019
, Adrianna,048 ,050
, Andrew,011,012,039,040
, Anne Maria,008,043
, Christina,010
, Daniel,034
, Dorothy,039
, Elisa,011
, Elisabeth,013 ,035
, George,035
, J.M.(Capt),054
, J.W.(Capt),020,026,055
, John,042
, Joseph,004,042
, Magdalen,039
, Margaret,034 ,039
, Martin,004,006,007,043
, Mary,012 ,040,057
SELLERS, Rebecca,013
, Rosina,042
, Samuel,006
, William,013
, Wm.(Mrs),043
SHAEFFER, W.C.(Rev),026
SHECK, J.D.(Rev),029,030
SHEPHERD, Ludwig,005
SHILLING, Robert,035,057
SHINGLER, George,043
, Martha C.,040
SHIRER, Aaron,036 ,040
, Adam,018,036
, Ann(Houser),018
, Ann,036
, John A.,022
, Mary Ann,017,022
, Mary,005,017
, Paul,005,043
, William D.,022
SHIRLNIGHT, Elizabeth,016
SHIRMER, (Mr),030
SHOKER, G.(Rev.),002
SHULER, (Mrs),062 ,064
, Adriana,048
, Adrianna,050
, Amanda C.,051
, Amanda,051
, Ann,040
, E.(Mrs),025
, J.L.(Dr),051
, J.L.,051
, Mary Rebecca,051
, Nancy(C),064
, Sarah,041
, Thos.Houck,051
SHULL, Mary,009
SHUMALLER, Frank,054
SHURLNIGHT, Albert J.,036
SHURLOUGH, A.J.,023
, Elizabeth,023
, Jane Eliz.,023
SIPHRET, Mary,058
SLATER, Anne,009
, Edmon,007
, Jane,009,043
, John,034,058
, Thomas,044
, William(Mast.),042
SLATOR, William,007
SLAUGHTEMYER, Eliz.,014
SLAVE, Ahrrsitta,063
, Abram,063
, Agga,025
, Agnes,064

, Agness,062
, Alex.Whitfield,025
, Amanda,025
, Amaritta,025
, Amelia,025
, Amey,066
, Amy,062 ,063,064
, Andy Isaac,062
, Ann,025
, Anna,062,063,066
, Bella,062
, Betty,063,066
, Bill,062
, Bob,063 ,066
, Captain,066
, Caroline,064
, Carson,064
, Cate,062
, Catherine,025
, Charles,062 ,066
, Chloe,025
, Dennis,062
, Elisabeth,064
, Ellick,062
, Fibby,063
, Francis Ann E.,062
, Frank,062
, Friday,062
, Gabriel,062
, Ginny,062
, Hallew,063
, Harriet,063
, Harriot,066
, Henry,063
, Hester,025
, Hetty,063,066
, Hiliard,025
, Isaac,066
, Jack,062,066
, Jacob,064
, James Noah,025
, James Seipio,062
, Jane Martha,025
, January,064
, Jeffery,063 ,066
, Jeremiah,025
, Jim,062
, Jinney,066
, Jock,064
, John Francis,062
, John,025,064,066
, Joseph Mosses,025
, Joseph,064
, July,066
, Karianne,025
, Katy,063,066
, Knight,065
, Lavina,025 ,062
, Lavinia,064
, Lebedee,063
, Lorron,025
, Louisa,062 ,064
, Lovely,062
, Lovey,025,063,064
, Lucy,025,062,063,066
, Manual,062
, Manuel,063 ,066
, Margaret,063,066
SLAVE, Maria,062
, Mariah,064
, Martha,062
, Mary Eliz.,062
, Mary Milley,066
, Mary,064,066
, Miley,063
, Milly,066
, Moses,063,066
, Myers,063
, Nancy,025,064
, Nanny,063,066
, Paul,063,066
, Peggy,063,066
, Peter,064
, Phillis,062 ,063
, Polly,025
, Primus,025
, Priscilla,066
, Rias Samuel,062
, Richard,025

, Rins,063
, Rius,025
, Robbin,066
, Robert,062   ,063,066
, Roxena,063   ,064,066
, Rozena,062
, Sally,063,066
, Sarah Ann,062,064
, Sarah,064,066
, Sary,062
, Seley Elvina,062
, Senipy,063
, Silvy,063,066
, Sonny,066
, Sophia,025
, Sophiah,066
, Syley,062
, Sylvia,025
, Tack,066
, Teaner,063
, Tiller,063
, Tinny,063
, Tobby,066
, Tuck,063
, Tuly,063
, Vicy,062
, Wade Sheppard,062
, Walley,063   ,066
, Wiley,025
, William,066
, Winny,066
, Zebbo,063
, Zebedee,025
SLOUGHTEMYER, Ann,014
SMITH, Adam,091,092
, Bishop,096
, Charles,039
, E.Manly,024
, Emeline,039
, Jacob,009,024,072,075,077
         ,081,084,091,092,094
, Margaret,044
, Mary,040
, W.Dorson,024
, Wm.James,009
SMOAK, Adam,010
, Anne,011
, Carolina,011
, George ,011
, John,010
SMOKE, Ann,016 ,017
, David,018,036
, Margaret,016,017
, Rebecca,018 ,036
SNEIDER, John,042
SNELL, Adam,091,095,096
SNIDER, Anne,034,039
, Catherine,034
, Elisabeth,034   ,039,060
, Elizabeth,016   ,018,057,
               059
, Jacob,057
, Margaret,039,043
, Mary,016,061
, William,058
SNYDER, Elizabeth,017
, Margrett,085
, Nancy,014
SOUDENMIRE, Barbara,060
SPEIGNARD, Geo.,010
, Rosina,034   ,039
, Simeon,010
SPIGNER, Catharine(C) ,064
STABLER, Alexander,009
, Andrew,004,005
, Ann,058
, Anne,006
, Catherine,005
, Chn.,009
, Christian,007
, Christina A.,009
, E.(Mrs),042
, Elisabeth,005
, Eliza,044
, Fred,006
, Fredk.,009
, George,042
, Harriet,009

, Jacob,004 ,009
, John,004
, Maria,006
, Mary,004
, Samuel,007
STACY, (Mast.),044
STEINWINDER, Alexr.,007
, Frederick,004
, Fredk.,005,007
, Mary,005
, Rachell,004
STELLINGER, Sarah,019
, Thomas,019
STENT, (Mr) ,077,079,081,085
STENT, William,078
, Wm.,074 ,075,076,078,080,
              083,085,087
STERLING, Henry,027
STEVENSON, Peter,082,086
STIDER, John Joseph,012
, John,012
STIFFELMYER, (Mast.),042
, Adam,010 ,043
, Catherine,010
, Elisabeth,034
, John,010 ,011
, Thomas,034
, Wm.David,011
STIFFLEMIRE, Elizabeth,058
, John C.,058
STIFFLEMYER, Elisabeth,012
, Eve,014
, Jno.,008
, John Henry,012
, Rosina,008
STILLINGER, Daniel,058
, Elizabeth H.,021
, John J.D.,021
, Martha J.E.,021
, S.(Mrs),021
, Sarah,019 ,038
, T.,021
, Thomas,021 ,038
STONE, Margaret,016,017,060
, Mary,016
, Rebecca,061
, Rebecca,016 ,017
STOUDENMEYER, David,018
, Mary,017
STOUDENMIRE, Adam,057
, Adriana,019
, Adrianna,048
, Barbara,016
, Charles,026,059,060
, Charlotte,016
, Chas.,015
, Daniel,057
, David,018
, Elizabeth,061
, Euganah,060
, Henry,059 ,060
, Martin,059
, Mary,016 ,018,058
, Mathias,057
STOUDENMYER, Charles,017,022
, David,022 ,036,046
, Mary Ann E.,022
, Mary Ann Eliza,046
, Mary,022   ,046
, Nancy E.,022
, S.B.,022
STOURENMYER, John,006
STOUTEMYER, Eugenia,013
STOUTENMEYER, John Martin,004
, Maria,004
, Martin,004
, Mathias,004
STOUTENMIRE, Catharine,059
STOUTENMYER, (Mast.),042
, Ann Elisa,012
, Anne,034 ,039
, Barb.,007
, Barbara,006,045
, Catherin,034
, Catherine,009
, Daniel,012,035,039
, David Martin,012

, Elisabeth,006
, Ellen,040
, Geo.,006 ,007
, Hannah,006
, Jacob,010 ,039,043
, Jane,034 ,039
, Jas.Joseph,012
, Jennett,005,007,039
, John M.,007
, John,005 ,007,039,
           043
, Juliana,007,043
, Ludwig,034
, Magdelen,035   ,039
, Margaret,010 ,039,
             040
, Maria L.,006
, Maria,042
, Mary C.B.,011
, Mat,006,009,011,013
, Mathias,007,010,012
, Nuel,005
, R.(Miss),042
, Rosina,034,039
, William,010
, Wm.James,006
STOUTERMYER, Rosina(Mrs),043
STROMAN, Catherine,040
, David Hope,046
, John,042
, Joshua,037
, Leah,037
, Louisa S. ,060
, Louisa(N.?),016
, Mary Ann,036
, N.,015
, Nicholas,015 ,046,061
, Selena,046
STROUDENMIRE, Mary,016
STRUBLE, John Jos.,010
STUART, (Mr),103
, James(Mr),105
, James,106 ,107
SWAIN, J.P.,045
SWITZER, ,066
, Elisabeth,008
, Elizabeth,026 ,058
, Frederick,026 ,058
, H.,008
, Henry,005 ,007,026,058
SWITZER, John R.,057
, John,034
, Magdelen,034 ,039
, Margaret,034 ,057
, Mary,026   ,034,057
, Samuel,005
SYFRID, John Jacob,007
, Thomas,007 ,043
SYFRIED, Thomas,042

TATE, John,099
, Samuel(Col),088   ,091
, Samuel,086,090
TAYLOR, Mary Ella,050
TEISS, (Dr),028
THEUS, Michial,004
, Simon,004
THOMASON, Chrissie,006
, Dorothy,006
THOMPSON, Wm.,071 ,073
THOMSON, (Col),085
, (Mr),085
, ,115
, Anne,035
, C.,119
, C.R.,108 ,109,119,120
, Charles,106
, Chas.,106
, Chas.R.,107,110,111,113
         ,115,116,117,118
, E.(Mrs),111,115,120
, E.,103
, Elizabeth(Mrs),110
, Elizabeth,107 ,118
, J.P.,092 ,093,097,098
, Jno.L.,107
, John Paul,091

, John,075   ,078
, W.J.,101   ,102,103
, W.L.,102
, W.R.,094   ,096,097
, W.T.,103   ,105,106,110,
         119,120
, William,073
, Wm.(Col),088   ,096
, Wm.,074,075,076,078,079
       ,082,084,085,091,091
       ,092,101
, Wm.J.,099 ,100,108
, Wm.R.,090   ,095
, Wm.S.,099 ,109
, Wm.T.(Col),115
, Wm.T.,107 ,108,109,111,
       113,114,115,116,117
TILL, Emmaly V.,041
, Irvin,040
, John,038 ,041
, Mary Ann,040
TILLEY, (Rev),028
TILLY & DANTZLER, ,002
TOLIN, Ellin,060
TREZEVANT, A.S.(Mr.&Mrs),055
          , D.,064
TREZEVEND, Ida C.(Mrs),054
TREZVANT, Ida C.,050
TROUTMAN, Rachel,009
TURQUAND, (Rev),073,075,076,079,
           084,086
         , Paul(Rev),089
         , Paul,072
ULMER, (Miss),043
     , (Mrs),015
     , Barbara,009
     , Cath.,009
     , Fredk.,009
     , Geo.,055
     , Milton,037
     , Rachel,059
     , William,037
UTZ, Abner,011
   , Geo.,011
VANCE, (Maj),099,103
     , (Mr),100
     , Moses,080
     , Wm.,098 ,099,099
VICE, Hannah,002
VISE, George,022
    , John D.F.,022
    , M.,022
    , Mary Dardes,016
    , Mary Dorcas,017
WALKER, Bill(C),064
      , Wesley(C),064
WALL, William,089
WALLING, David A.,020, ,038,050
       , David(Mrs),054
       , David,054
       , John David,056
       , Rose Ella,056
WALTS, Morgan J.,052
WALTZ, Alice Ann,050,052,054
     , Casper,004 ,035
     , Casr.,006
     , Charlie,056
     , Clarence,056
     , Conrad,004
     , Hattie(Mrs.Jos.),054
     , Isabella,046
     , Jacob C.,046
     , John Nichols,055
     , John,046
     , M.W.,047
     , Margaret,037
     , Marion Wash.M.,047
     , Martha A.,050,054
     , Martha Angeline,052
     , Mary,006,034
     , Morgan J.,050
     , Morgan,054
     , Sarah,050,052,054
     , W.M.,053
     , William M.,050
     , Wm.(Mr.&Mrs),055
WALTZ, Wm.(Mrs),054
     , Wm.,054

WANAMAKER, Rebecca,037
WANNAMACKER, Martin N.,009
WANNAMAK, Eugena,040
WANNAMAKER, (C),064
          , Ann,059
          , Anne E.,010
          , E.,008
          , Elisabeth,009 ,010
          , Elizabeth,015 ,017,
            058
          , Eugena,015
          , Jacob,008 ,009,010
          , Margaret,008
WANNAMEKER, Margaret,026
WANNEMAKER, Elizar,041
WARLEY, (Mrs),119
      , ,092
      , Paul,094
      , T.,115
WARNE, David,035
WATT, Ann E.,016,017,018
    , Ann,018 ,036,060
    , Elizabeth,022
    , Frances Irena,022
    , William,018 ,022,089
    , Wm.,017 ,089,090
WATTS, (Capt),088
     , John,004
     , Robert,004
     , William,061
     , Wm.,016
WEAKS, Mary,060
WEEKS, Harmon,040
     , Mary Ann,018,040
WEILS, Caroline,017
     , James,018
WEIMER, Daniel,041
      , Mary C.,041
WEIS, (Mr),042
    , Magdalen,010
    , Magdelen,039
    , Mary,004 ,034
    , Wm.Jacob,010
WEISSENHAND, Anne,012
           , Catherine,012
           , George,012
WELLS, Catherine,039
     , Robert,039
WEST, George(Mast.),042
    , George,004
    , Mary,035 ,058
WHETSTONE, C.,002
         , Jacob,039
         , Magdelen,039
         , Margaret,061
         , Mary,039
         , Rebecca,039
WHITE, Ann,039
     , Elizabeth,039
WHITEMAN, (Mr.),044
WILD, Adam,034
    , Rachell,043
WILES, (Child),055
     , Adam,057,061
     , Caroline,040
     , Carrie Elizabeth,055
     , Catherine,020,048,049,050
     , Emanuel,018 ,019,037
     , Hariott,061
     , Harriet R.,016
     , James,036,040
     , John,014,059
     , Peter Edward,014
     , Ugenia Katherine,014
     , W.(Mrs),020
     , W.W.(Mr.&Mrs.),055
     , W.W.,054
     , Walter,056
     , Wesley Walter,052
     , Wesley,020 ,052
WILLEN, Robt,071
      , Robt.,074 ,075
WILLIAMS, Adeline,040
WILSON, (Mr),118
      , (Rev),020
      , J.H.(Rev),026 ,051,053
      , William T.,117
      , Wm.L.(Rev),111

WINGARD, A.A.,054
       , Hetty E.,041
       , Jacob(Rev),029
       , John,003
       , Mary C.,041
       , Mary E.(Mrs),054
       , Mary Louise,003
       , Sarah N.,003
WINGART, Absolom,035
       , Christina,035
       , Salome,035
WISE, Adam,044
    , Cebastian,057
    , Darkes,060
    , George,034,057
    , John N.(Rev),026
    , Margaret,058
    , Mary,015
WISENHUNT, Catherine,053
         , Mary Ann,019
WISSENGER, Mathias,035
WISSENHUNT, Anna,038,050
          , Anne,034
          , Catherine,016 ,017,
            018,019,040,050
          , Eliza,061
          , Frances M.,019 ,041
          , Frances U.,038
          , George,018 ,034,037,
            040
          , Mary,015
          , William,035
WISSINHUNT, Catherine,022 ,048
WISSINHUNT, David J.,022
          , Mary Ann C.,022
WISSNEHUNT, Jane E.,050
WITTEN, Peter,096
WOLF, Catherine,016
    , E.(Mrs),063
    , Frederick,015
    , H.,062
WOLFE, (Mrs),064
     , ,066
     , Ann,047
     , Catharine,045
     , Catherine Holman,046
     , Catherine,046
     , Eleanor,056
     , Ella,040
     , Ellen,017,018
     , Martha C.,019,038,048,050
     , Martha(Miss),054
     , T.H.,045,046
     , Texas,040
     , W.W.(Dr),054
     , Walter(Dr),050 ,053
     , Wiley,040
     , Wm.Mack,054
WOLRICH, John,084
WORLEY, (Mr),088
      , Thos.,118
WOTTEN, Elisabeth,040
      , John,040
WYSE, Henrietta C.,048
ZAHAN, Jacob C.,086
ZAHN, Jacob X.,087
ZAHU, J.C.,086
    , Jac(?),085
    , Jacob C.,080 ,082
ZEAGLER, A.G.,017
       , Alex,036
       , Jos.G.,017
       , Mary Ann,017
       , Mary,036 ,040
ZIEGLER, (Mrs),042
       , A.,006
       , Andrew,004
       , Ann,042
       , Aw.,008
       , Carolina,044
       , Caroline,011
       , Catherine,006 ,043
       , David,004 ,005
       , E.,008
       , Elisabeth,010
       , Elizabeth,034
       , Frances,044
       , Francis,008

```
        , Geo.,005    ,007,008,009,
            010
        , Geo.Alexr.,011
        , George,011,039
        , Jacob(Mast.),044
        , Jacob,009   ,010,012,013,
            039
        , John Andw.,013
        , John,005    ,007,008,010,
            039,044
        , Joseph G.,036
        , Josiah,009
        , Magdalen,005
        , Margaret,012   ,039
        , Maria,007
        , Nicolas,010
        , R.,008
        , Rachel,011,034,039
        , Racheli,010,011
        , Rosina,039
        , Sarah,009
ZIGLER, (Miss),044
ZIMMERMAN, ,043
        , Adam,004
        , Adriana(Tilley),019
        , Anna A.,019
        , Anna R.(Mrs),054
        , Anna R.,019   ,038,048,
            050
        , Barbara,034
        , Catherine,042
        , Daniel,005    ,006,035
        , Elisabeth,005,006,018
        , Eliz.,015
        , Elizabeth,017,019,022
            ,026,047,048,050
        , Ella,040
        , Hannah,005
        , Henry,057
        , John Conrad,006
        , John,004
        , Margaret,057
        , Mary,034,057
        , Pashly,042
        , R.,062
        , R.H.,019,026,048,049,
            050
        , Russel D.,022
        , Russel H.,018,036,037
            ,047
        , Russel,002    ,018,022,
            025,056
        , Russell D.,050   ,054
        , Sophia,039
        , William(Mast.),043
        , William,005
ZUBLY, Joachim,027
```

www.ingramcontent.com/pod-product-compliance
Lightning Source LLC
Chambersburg PA
CBHW020656300426
44112CB00007B/398